Children and the Christian Faith

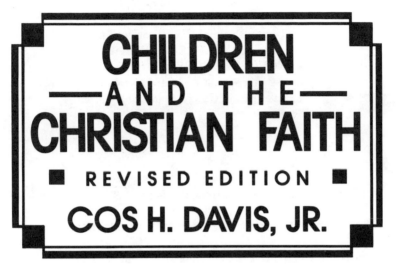

CHILDREN
—AND THE—
CHRISTIAN FAITH
■ REVISED EDITION ■
COS H. DAVIS, JR.

BROADMAN PRESS
Nashville, Tennessee

© Copyright 1979, 1990 • Broadman Press
All rights reserved
4262-21
ISBN: 0-8054-6221-X

Dewey Decimal Classification: 649
Subject Headings: CHILDREN - RELIGIOUS LIFE //
EVANGELISTIC WORK WITH CHILDREN
Library of Congress Catalog Card Number: 89-37252
Printed in the United States of America

All Scripture references are from the *Revised Standard Version of
the
Bible,* copyrighted 1946, 1952, ©1971, 1973.

Library of Congress Cataloging-in-Publication Data
Davis, Cos H.
    Children and the Christian Faith / Cos H. Davis, Jr.-- Rev. ed.
    p. cm.
    ISBN: 0-8054-6221-X :
    1. Christian education of children. 2. Family--Religious life.
I. Title.
BV1475.2.D38 1990
248.8'45--dc20
                                                                89-37252
                                                                    CIP

To Geneva and Cos H. Davis, Sr.,
loving parents who were always
there when I needed them.

Contents

I
The Parents' Role in Religious Training

1

Responsible but Inadequate

Parents often feel inadequate to do many of the things which they ought to do for their children. Religious instruction would certainly be in that ought-to-but-inadequate category. The mixture of ought-to-but-inadequate often results in such a request as this: "Pastor, I need your help! Sissy, my nine-year-old daughter, has been asking lots of questions which I don't know how to answer. Do you think you might be able to talk with her this week?"

There may be brief comfort in knowing that most parents do not feel at ease discussing the religious inquiries of their children. As a matter of fact, some evade or ignore the issue completely. Such comfort is short-lived for Christian parents who feel that the spiritual growth of their child is primarily their responsibility but do not know how to go about helping the child.

How much better it would be for both children and parents if parents would voice this request: "Pastor, I need your help! Sissy, my nine-year-old daughter, has been asking lots of questions which I don't know how to answer. Could you help me so that I may help her?"

How good it is for parents to be able to rely on the pastor or staff member at such a crucial time. But how much better for the parents to become directly involved in the conversion and spiritual growth of their child! Parents, you can do it. Think about some of the reasons why you should become involved in the spiritual growth of your child. You will likely decide that you can do it; you must do it.

How Much Is He Worth

Most parents agree that their children are priceless. Most parents also agree that there are those frustrating moments when they would almost give their children away. How winsome, precious, and disturbing children can be!

Even our most prejudiced attempt at putting a value on our children will result in an inadequate estimation of their true worth. The real value of a child can only be assessed in terms of the gospel of Jesus Christ. Each child, and every human being for that matter, is to be viewed in terms of what God has done to save him . God has determined that each child is worth a Calvary. John 3:16 is more than a beautiful sentiment we teach our children to voice. It expresses the literal truth regarding God's esteem for them.

If we sense the depth of God's love for our children, we will conclude that it is tremendously important for them to understand who Jesus is and to trust Him as Savior. One of the greatest joys in the lives of parents is to lead their children to that expression of faith in Jesus.

Moral Accountability

There comes a point of time in the child's life when he becomes responsible before God. There is no certain, specific age when this occurs. Rather, it is that period when the child can discriminate between right and wrong and is aware of his failure to always do that which is right and to always refrain from that which is wrong. The child's inner response is one of feeling guilt, though he cannot identify his feeling as one of guilt.

It is difficult for most of us to accept the fact of sin in the lives of our children. We can much more readily admit to our failures as adults. But sin is a reality with our children too. They realize its power is present even if we refuse to do so. The fact of sin is there and must be dealt with.

If a child has reached the stage of maturity where he is morally responsible, he is also accountable to God for his sins. Without Christ, he is lost. John 3:18 tells us: "He who believes in him is not condemned; he who does not believe is condemned already, because he has not believed in the name of the only Son of God."

If we believe that the Bible is true concerning the dilemma of those who are lost, we as parents should want to give correct guidance when our children reach that crucial point in their lives. Being prepared to help when that time comes can be helpful to your child and most satisfying to you.

Spiritual Growth

Children grow. Much to the amazement of parents, and often to their dismay, children grow rapidly. With every passing day, their dependency upon parents is becoming more a thing of the past. Like it or not, that is as it should be.

Spiritual growth, however, is not nearly as predictable or assured as other types of growth in children. The neglect or ignorance of the principles of spiritual growth may explain why some people are chronologically mature but are still in their spiritual infancy. They act in childish ways as far as God and others are concerned.

The goal of the Christian life is capsuled in the phrase: "conformed to the image of his Son" (Rom. 8:29). As parents, we have much to do with all areas of our children's growth, including the spiritual. Certainly we want the best in terms of those things which influence their physical, mental, and social lives. The best life has to offer is found in a growing relationship to Jesus Christ. If we have been instrumental in our children's decisions to trust Christ, we will more than likely be called upon to assist and to advise in areas related to spiritual development.

Parents Are Responsible

While most of us will confess that we feel woefully inadequate to guide our children in their spiritual pilgrimages, we also concede that such is our responsibility. That sense of obligation is why we seek out those who are especially trained in Christian ministry. That is why we read such books as this. We are aware and concerned, but we need help.

The concept of parental responsibility in the religious instruction of children is a biblical one. The Shema, Deuteronomy 6:4-7, was the primary religious tenet among the Hebrews. Such an important and lofty concept of God was to be passed on to the young Hebrew children so they might know it from their early years. Whom did God designate as responsible to instruct children in this concept of faith? Parents are responsible. A reading of Deuteronomy 6:7 leaves no doubt: "You shall teach them diligently to your children, and shall talk of them when you sit in your house, and when you walk by the way, and when you lie down, and when you rise."

Much to their credit, many of the Hebrews consciously used the sounds, sights, and activities of the home to teach religious truth. The home was viewed as the primary educational agency for hundreds of years, and parents were the teachers of their children.

Jesus and Paul were doubtless reared in the tradition which stressed the spiritual influence and instruction of the home. Timothy had also benefited greatly from the Christian instruction he received in his home. Paul's reference, in 2 Timothy 1:5, to the faith of Lois and Eunice, Timothy's grandmother and mother, is a reminder of the wholesome influence home had on Timothy's development.

There are other reasons why parents are responsible. Parents are obviously the most effective teachers a child will ever have. The young child depends upon parents for almost everything he learns. From a very early age, he learns about his value and the value of other people and things. As he grows older, his circle of associates expands. He, naturally, learns many things from them. Nevertheless, there is no influence so profound or so enduring as that of the parent. For good or bad, parents, through their constant examples and words, are a child's most effective teachers.

The home is also the most natural environment for teaching religious truth to children. Where else in all the world is a better setting to teach about faith, personal relationships, responsibility, stewardship, and love? Furthermore, the blending of religion and life in the home helps us avoid a serious division which is often made between the spiritual and the secular. Faith in Christ is not merely something expressed in a church building on Sunday. Christ lives in the life of the believer and is with him everywhere. The atmosphere and routine of the home should reflect this. Talking to God and about God should be as normal as any other part of daily life. There is no place in the child's experience which is so endowed with potential for learning about God as his home.

It is generally true that the concern, or lack of it, which parents show will determine the depth to which children become involved in the fellowship and Bible teaching of a local church. Needless to say, parents who are deeply concerned about the spiritual aspect of their children's lives are usually actively involved in a church. An appreciation for the role the church can play in the spiritual growth of children can be an asset which parents can provide for children who are on spiritual quests.

My purpose for writing this chapter has been to increase your sense of responsibility as your child's spiritual guide. If you have entered upon this experience feeling deficient in this area, you have likely sensed an increase in the level of your anxiety. Feeling responsible but inadequate creates a certain amount of tension in all of us.

Tension can be creatively helpful! Make your sense of concern work for you. Change that concept of "responsible but inadequate" to "responsible and adequate." A prayerful study of the following chapters will better equip you to serve as the guide on your child's most meaningful adventure of life.

2

A Perspective on Child Conversion

Experiences of our childhood often affect the way we relate to our own children. This is true, for good or bad, regarding methods of discipline, self-esteem, values, and religious instruction. Once an adult has weighed the alternate ways in which something can be approached he has more freedom to make a valid choice as to what course to follow with his own child. This chapter is written to help you grapple with some ideas and influences which have been part of your understanding of child conversion to this point. Hopefully, you will know more about where you really stand on this issue once you have completed these next few pages.

The Parents' Dilemna

Do you believe in childhood conversion? If you were asked this question, you perhaps would respond with an affirmative nod. But you would probably hasten to point out that you have your doubts about very young children being converted. The subject becomes more intensely complex when the question is: How would you feel if *your* child expressed concern about being converted? *My* child! That's different, isn't it?

When it is your child who is interested in accepting Jesus, you are faced with a dilemma. The problem is how to guide your child without being either too restricting or too encouraging. What makes this balance so difficult to achieve?

Conflicting philosophies. These are many different views of child evangelism and the spiritual status of the child. Some church groups believe in and practice infant baptism as a means of atoning for original sin. Some groups manipulate and push young children into public decisions while others take a completely hands-off position. There is no one clearly defined view of child conversion by the Christian denominations and churches of the world. Then, how do parents decide where they really stand on the matter?

Personal experiences. Your personal experience of the way your parents dealt with your religious concerns when you were a child may greatly color your perspective about your role. For instance, your parents may have held you back from making your public decision until you almost lost interest. You may feel that you were denied making a decision for which you were ready. On the other hand, your parents may have shown little concern about what you did. Or, they may have been a bit on the pushy side, causing you later to wonder if your decision was really yours or theirs. Such influences may make the achievement of balance more difficult as we relate to our children about conversion.

Personal involvement. An ever-present hazard is the lack of objectivity. This is true of almost all areas of our children's experiences. We are so deeply involved in their lives that it is often difficult to approach the subject with objectivity and fairness. It is difficult to believe that Johnny isn't a baby anymore even though he protests that our perspective needs to be changed. How it challenges us to believe that our little girl, who was a toddler only yesterday, is really old enough to be considering a profession of faith. Other children her age are making such decisions, but she just doesn't seem old enough yet.

Lack of understanding of conversion. As much as we hate to admit it, our problem may be partially due to a lack of understanding of what is involved in conversion. We have never really stopped to think through the simple process of the miracle of conversion. Maybe we are making something much too complicated out of it. Perhaps we are looking on it as purely the work or accomplishment of a human being. Review your own experience with Christ, and you will discover that it is a childlike faith which claims the promises of Christ.

Expecting too much. We often labor under the false impression that conversion has to be dramatic in nature. We tend to look for standard signs by which we judge the depth of a person's experience. On the contrary, two people may respond emotionally in two radically different ways to the experience of conversion. One may weep while another may laugh with joy. The difference? People are different and respond individually to the saving grace of Jesus. Should you expect a child with little experience in gross sins to react in the same manner as a wicked man who is converted? There is a change in the child at conversion, to be sure, but there is not usually the deep emotional upheaval which may accompany many adult conversions.

Can a Child Believe?

On one occasion in our Lord's ministry, parents were eagerly bringing their children to Jesus that He might touch them. The disciples discouraged such attempts by the parents, perhaps feeling that Jesus was too busy for the children. The Gospel of Mark records that the Master became indignant with the disciples and said: "Let the children come to me, do not hinder them; for to such belongs the kingdom of God. Truly, I say to you, whoever does not receive the kingdom of God like a child shall not enter it" (Mark 10:14-15).

Obviously, Jesus makes the attitude of the child toward Himself, not that of the adult, the standard for entering the kingdom. It is precisely the curious, trusting, humble disposition of young children which enables them to perceive so much of the truth that has grown dim or vanished completely to the adult.

Certainly a child can believe. But how much or how deeply? He cannot believe as deeply or intellectually as can an adult. Neither can he understand the same content. But he can believe with all the faith that is within him. And Christ honors such faith which is placed in Him. Jesus' concern was not with whether a child could trust Him but with whether an adult would trust Him as a child is capable of doing.

Responsible and Accountable

Our personal understanding of people and their relationship to God has much to do with how we approach child conversion in general and the instruction of our children in particular. Your answer to the following questions will help you clarify your thoughts.

—Does a an individual have an ability to distinguish right from wrong?

—Is sin the initial choice of all who can make a choice between good and evil?

—Are individuals accountable to God for their sins? The Bible teaches that the answer to each of these questions is affirmative. Yes, human beings can make moral choices. Yes, human beings do choose to sin against God. And, yes, human beings are accountable to God for their sins or trespasses against God's law.

As parents, the question with which we must wrestle concerning our children is: When do they become lost? The answer is quite simple: They become lost when they become responsible for their own moral decisions. The difficult part is to know or recognize just when that time comes. We should remember that condemnation comes as a result of rejecting Jesus as Savior (see John 3:16-21).

What, then, is the child's status before he becomes responsible? There is no Bible verse or passage which deals directly with this question. However, we can deduce from the general teachings of the Scriptures that God is loving and just and can be trusted to deal graciously toward our children. After all, conversion or condemnation is based upon a person's ability to accept or reject Jesus as Savior. It is my opinion that our Lord would no more condemn a child who could not believe than He would save a person who refused to believe.

Foundations

My willingness to believe that my child is safe before he is accountable does not mean that I should wait until he becomes accountable to begin trying to help him. On the contrary, the parents' job is to lay foundations for faith in Christ, so the child may respond to Christ in a meaningful way at an early age. We cannot get away from the idea that parents are the teachers of religious values and concepts. It is our task to teach our children to respect God as Creator and Redeemer, to love others as themselves, and to obey God's rules for living. If such teachings are conveyed by examples, as well as by precept, we may be assured that we have done much to guide our children toward a genuine acceptance of Jesus as Savior.

3
Pros and Problems of Childhood Conversion

Some people seem to think that the only benefits of con version come after death. Is Christian conversion nothing more than a "ticket to heaven" or "fire prevention"? Do such concepts really miss or minimize the daily values of such an experience? While there is a future aspect and value to conversion, there are present, meaningful realities as well.

In the next few pages we will look at some of the positive values and possible problems for everyday living which may be found in the life of the child who has experienced Christian conversion. This is not an exhaustive treatment of the subject but a good beginning place.

Values of Childhood Conversion
Life of Service

Childhood conversion has value through time. The child has the possibility of a long life of service to Christ. Life's primary purpose is to honor and to serve Christ. The young convert has a lifetime to devote to Him who is at the center of life's purpose and meaning.

It is truly a wonderful miracle for an adult to experience conversion, but there is the remorse of years and energies spent in pursuit of goals not related to Christ's will. The conversion of a child holds the promise of a lifetime lived for Christ. This is the greater miracle!

Life Unmarred by Sin

The child convert also has the possibility of a life unmarred by the effects of gross sin. While there will be sin in the life of any believer, there are the restraints which, if followed, will keep the believer from activities and involvements which will be harmful to the body and mind. There is less likely, for the person who attempts to follow Christ from an early age, the possibility of physical and emotional scars caused by such things as adultery, alcohol, and drugs.

Sin has its price. God forgives sin, but He does not erase the evil effect or damage sin has brought to its victim. What a wonderful thing to see persons grow to maturity without the physically and emotionally devastating effects of sin in their lives.

Sense of Direction

One of the tragedies of life is never to find meaning and purpose in living. Life's search for meaning takes many directions: materialism, drugs, sex, alcohol, pleasure, and religion. None of these is meaningful in a permanent sense.

The child who is converted has opportunity, at an early age, to come into vital contact with the Source of life and the Purpose of life. Jesus is that source and purpose, as Paul explained in Colossians 1:16-17: "All things were created through him and for him. He is before all things, and in him all things hold together."

Life's deep secrets and purposes are found in Jesus Christ and those who know Him have access to the meaning and purpose of life. Is this not implied in Jesus' statement in John 14:6, "I am the way, and the truth, and the life" ? How fortunate is the person who finds such purpose in his early years!

Spiritual Security

It is not unusual for children to have fears related to dying and going to hell. The fear motive to receive Christ is often used to pressure children and others into making decisions. Hell is a reality, but escape of hell is not, in itself, a proper motive for trusting Christ. If this is the only basis for a decision, the decision is probably not genuine. Such dread or fear is often involved in a child's decision.

Conversion does bring a release of the fear of hell to the child. The child senses that she and God are no longer enemies. How marvelous such peace is!

More Cooperative at Home

Children who are Christians should prove to be more cooperative at home. We should not expect an overnight change in behavior and attitudes, but improvement should be evidenced in home relationships. The young child usually identifies herself as a sinner in ways which relate to family relationships. For instance, she may admit that she has lied or been disobedient or disrespectful to parents. She will likely also admit to mistreating a brother or sister. Given time and encouragement, more responsible patterns of behavior ought to emerge in the life of the child.

The child needs to be reminded that she belongs to the Lord and that the Lord holds her responsible for her relationships. Look at Exodus 20:12 and Ephesians 6:1-3 for biblical teachings on this subject.

Parental Security

The conversion of our children has benefits to us as parents. One such value is the knowledge of our children's relationship to Christ. Parents are sometimes concerned, and rightly so, about what would be the spiritual destiny of their children if the children should die in their present spiritual state.

Many parents have agonized over their children's spiritual condition until they were certain conversion had taken place. Such a knowledge brings release and joy to the parents who have been prayerfully concerned about their children's spiritual destiny.

There is perhaps no comfort so real to Christian parents as that which comes with the knowledge that their child has been converted. What a deep sense of satisfaction to know that those to whom we have given physical birth and life have now begun to share with us in the new life which God gives!

Appreciation of Christian Values

Christian values are somehow related to most of the values of childhood conversion which have already been discussed. With the conversion of the child comes a changing of attitude toward what Christ desires. There is set in motion a struggle to overcome selfishness and a desire to please Christ. This desire to please Christ aids parents who are attempting to construct and to reinforce a set of values by which children are to live. Christian conversion involves the acceptance of Christ and His value system. Although conversion does not accomplish this immediately or automatically, it does make children teachable and receptive to such values. This is a big plus for parents.

Problems Related to Childhood Conversion

As odd as it may sound, there are problems related to childhood conversion. These problems are not encountered because of conversion itself, but because of the lack of guidance in certain areas. What are some of the problem areas of which we need to be aware?

Parental Letdown

One of the most discouraging things that can happen to children after conversion is for parents to feel that they have accomplished all that must be done. Parents who assume that their task is over when their children are converted show their lack of understanding concerning spiritual growth.

The conversion of our children is a wonderful thing, but it is just the beginning, not the end, of our children's spiritual journey. It will be disastrous if we, the children's guides, abandon them at the beginning of their quest. Parents are the single most important factor determining where children "end up" on their pilgrimage for life's meaning.

We read our newspapers in disgust and dismay at those

who will abandon a newborn child. Imagine a helpless baby having to survive on his own! Unless he is found soon after abandonment, he does not survive. There is an important parallel here for parents whose children have been converted.

Somewhere I ran across this idea: The new birth is the miracle of a moment, but the making of a saint is the work of a lifetime. That's worth thinking about, isn't it?

Doubts

I would say that later doubts about the validity of a childhood conversion is almost universal among children as they grow older. As children grow in their understanding, their broadening concepts of faith and other religious values make their earlier decisions seem too simple to be real. The problem is often due to the fact that children begin making knowledge, and not faith, the primary criterion by which to judge past experiences. This is an unfair judgment, one which could be used to discount a valid decision in one's youth if judged by adult knowledge.

Another promoter of doubts is the child's sins. She has a difficult time realizing that, though converted, the struggle with the problem of sin will continue. When she sins, she may feel that this only confirms her doubts that she was never really saved at all.

Parents need to be aware of the fact that many children, in later years, may doubt the validity and sincerity of their earlier decision. We can help by being alert and sympathetic and by reassuring them that their doubts are not proof of their fears but of the fact that they are alive and growing. We can also bring them back to the reality of their conversion by helping them see that we can trust Christ to do what He has promised to do. No matter what we feel, the truth is that we are saved through faith, not by our feelings.

A Void in Experience

Some childhood converts later wonder if they have not been cheated out of some life experiences because of their early conversion. This is purely a problem of speculation, but it can cause disillusionment in a child.

Most of us have grown up with the cultural influences which have said that such things as drinking, smoking, sex, and drugs are rather accepted and common experiences of childhood and youth. Our children are exposed to this culture, and such exposure may raise questions as to whether they have really missed anything.

This point involves a question of basic values. Do we really believe the best in life is found in relation to Jesus Christ? Does He really give abundant and meaningful life? Are His ways better than the ways of sin? Is a person harmed by not experiencing those things which are involved in degrading oneself and others? These are the issues. What is your answer?

4

Foundations for Faith

Life has a way of proving that the beginning or foundational stage of any endeavor is crucial to the final outcome. Egyptian pyramids, built thousands of years before Christ, stand along the Nile in silent testimony that their foundations received proper attention. Jesus closed the teachings of the Sermon on the Mount with a parable of the wise and foolish builders. Their wisdom or foolishness was determined by the foundation upon which each chose to build. Poets have also discerned the basic value of the beginning or foundational period of life. Alexander Pope wrote: "Just as the twig is bent the tree's inclined." William Wordsworth wrote: "The child is father of the man."

Pyramids, houses, and trees have something to say about life. Their message is quite clear. To be enduring and strong, a person must have proper foundations.

The Importance of Faith

Faith is one of the most basic elements of life. It is absolutely necessary for all of one's involvements, from the most mundane to the most sublime. For instance, a type of faith is necessary to sit in a chair, lie on a bed, drive a car, or to do countless other everyday things. In order to do all of these things, we must put ourselves in the care of that chair, bed, or car. We must trust it to do what it is supposed to do.

The same is true in human relationships. Faith is of paramount importance in building and maintaining good relationships. Marriage and family life cannot maintain its function apart from trust in each other. Friendships are impossible without trust.

One's relationship to God is also built upon faith. Hebrews 11:6 expresses the idea that in order to please God one must believe God exists and, further, that He approves those who seek His will. Ephesians 2:8 tells us that a saving relationship to God is the product of God's grace and our faith.

The biblical idea of saving faith involves commitment to, or trust in, God with a willingness to obey God. All persons are born with the possibility of expressing such faith, but the ability to do so can be developed or hindered in the foundational stages of life.

Need and Ability to Believe

By his very position in life, a child has a natural need to believe—to trust others. From the time of conception until he is grown, the child depends upon parents and other caregivers to do for him what he cannot do for himself. Thus, his physical, emotional, social, intellectual, and spiritual needs as a growing person dictate that he be able to trust someone else to help him in meeting these various needs. More than at any other stage or position in life, the child needs to trust others. What a tremendously important and beautiful thing to see a child's trust reinforced by those who conscientiously seek to meet his needs.

As awesome as the child's need to believe is her ability to believe. She is so sure that her parents can do everything needed that it disarms and humbles us. How simple and pure is her faith! She allows adults to worry about the details of meeting her needs, and she just believes they will do it. It takes her some time to realize that the absolute faith she has in us has been somewhat misplaced.

So often children are judged as immature because their bodies, actions, thought patterns, and concerns do not parallel those of the adult world. It is interesting to note, however, the strange reversal Jesus used to challenge those adults who would follow Him. Adult faith, so often filled with doubt and skepticism, was not the standard of trust Jesus used. The simple, unreserved faith children show toward their parents is the type of faith necessary to enter the kingdom of God. There is a wealth of meaning in such phrases as "turn and become like children" (Matt. 18:3) and "to such belongs the Kingdom of God" (Mark 10:14). Yes, Jesus is absolutely clear at the point of believing. An adult-type faith, with its reservations and skepticism, cannot approach the trust and humility necessary to enter the kingdom. Rather, says Jesus, "Whoever does not receive the kingdom of God like a child shall not enter it" (Mark 10:15).

A Child's First Faith

One of the most sobering thoughts that an adult could ever have is that the child's first faith is faith in the parent. What an awesome responsibility to be the first object of faith for a developing life.

Little children express this faith in many ways. A clap of thunder, and they may rush to your arms for protection. They let you know when they are wet or soiled, with the trust that you will take care of them. They simply assume that you will provide food and clothing. They also hope you will set limits to protect them from themselves and from things in the world which will harm them. All of these are expressions of the child's faith.

Developmental psychologists emphasize a sense of trust as the first of the developmental tasks which the child must achieve. This trust is developed as parents meet the basic needs of the child. For instance, feeding the child when she is hungry indicates that you care for her. She translates your response to her need into trust. At any level of development, meeting a child's needs helps her to trust you.

When one understands how the ability to trust is developed, it is not sacrilegious to say that the parent is the child's first god. Before a child ever conceives of the possibility of the idea of God, he believes only in his parents. They assume an intermediate role in his pilgrimage of faith in God.

Transfer of Faith

Parents, the first object of a child's faith, influence her ability to place trust in other persons and, ultimately, in God. The healthy child is ready to form friendships and to trust significant adults, such as a teacher, pastor, or doctor. As life expands and experiences multiply, the growing child will learn to use the faith she has been taught in all types of relationships.

Hopefully, there will come a time when this faith in parents will enable the child to place her faith in Jesus as Savior. Without her real awareness, the child's faith has been in the process of transfer from parent to Jesus for some time. The simple, trusting faith in parents is expressed toward Jesus as God and as supreme. Her growing awareness of parents as fallible people will no longer allow the child to completely trust them as God. But the transfer of this simple faith can be made to God, who is without fault. The best of parents have faults and are pleased to know that their children have put their trust in One who will not fail them.

While faith in Christ is not inherited as one would inherit a family heirloom, faith is learned and developed in relationship with significant others, such as parents. Timothy is an excellent example of one who came to faith in Christ out of a background of faith provided by his grandmother and mother. Paul's words continue to challenge parents today to provide the foundations for faith for our children: "I am reminded of your [Timothy's] sincere faith, a faith that dwelt first in your grandmother Lois and your mother Eunice and now, I am sure, dwells in you" (2 Tim. 1:5).

5

A Time to Speak

As parents, we sometimes find ourselves assuming the role of protector regarding our children. This is as it should be because our years, experience, and, hopefully, our wisdom are greater than theirs. We have learned, often the hard way, that not all persons, programs, or ideas have the best interest of our children in view.

We are careful, or should be, in the choice of a doctor for our children. We do not want just anyone caring for their physical health. The physician may be well intentioned and may like children, but he must know what he is doing. We do not want second-rate teachers influencing our children with shoddy preparation and destructive ideas. We should do all within our power to protect our children from such people.

It is sad but true that our children often need protecting from people who are trying to "save" them. There are many people seeking converts, and our children are prime targets for such individuals. Some parents are relieved to hear that their children have been "saved" and never question the motive or methods of those who "converted" them. I believe such decisions should be weighed by parents in light of certain motives or tactics involved

by those working with our children. Children may have
had valid conversion experiences. The point is not to deny
such experiences, but to determine if the prompting for
such an experience was people or the work of the Holy
Spirit.

What Is at Stake?

Attempting to determine the motive or method of those
who discuss spiritual things with our children is a deli-
cate matter. We run the risk of offending them by inquir-
ing about this involvement and what form it took. But we
must remember two things. First, it is the parents' duty
and right to show concern about such things. Second, asking for an explanation of procedure or methods is not
questioning the motive of the worker. It is an attempt to
determine how a child's decision came about.

If a person becomes offended by our inquiries, it is likely that the motive or method is suspect. We tend to act
most protectively concerning those things about which
we are unsure. It seems that there are three alternatives
facing the parent. First, act as if nothing has happened.
This assumes that nothing, in fact, has happened. But
something has happened, and it must be determined just
what that something is. Otherwise, the child may be con-
fused or may need guidance which is denied. Second, accept the decision at face value without question. Some
parents do this because they have been so prayerful for
their child's conversion and see this as an answer to their
prayers. But to question is not to doubt the power of God.
It is rather an attempt to determine if further prayer and
concern in this matter are needed. It is an effort to determine if this is the work of God in answer to our prayers.

Third, talk with the person who was involved with the child at the point of this decision. This is exercising our rights as parents and showing our concern. We should do this. Our children need for us to do this.

A Point of Concern

My several years in the pastorate and in personal contact with children have convinced me of some astounding facts. One of the most humbling is that children can be manipulated by a religious worker to make almost any type of decision. Why is this true?

First, it is true because children are usually taught to respect a pastor or other staff worker as an authority figure. It is difficult for a child to believe such a person could have a wrong idea or say or do anything which is inconsistent with the role.

Second, ministers often have a friendly and loving manner with children. They become special to children, and the children are intent upon pleasing them. Sometimes decisions can be made to win the approval of such a beloved worker.

Third, children are trusting and can be manipulated without great effort. They generally trust the motives of those who represent Jesus and will respond to most tactics or methods without question.

Motives and Methods

What kinds of motives and methods should make parents cautious for the sake of our children? Are there those persons who have selfish motives in promoting the conversion of our children? Is the old pragmatic philosophy "If it works, it's good" really acceptable?

Sometimes a personal need or selfish motive causes persons to influence unduly our children toward conversion. There are those who have records to keep untarnished, and children are made to feel guilty if they do not respond to Christ. For example, some Sunday School teachers pride themselves on the fact that each year all of the children in their classes make professions of faith. Such should be the interest of all teachers, but it should never be something which is a record-keeping or personal-accomplishment sort of thing. The danger involved is that the worker may begin to consciously or unconsciously pressure the "unbaptized" or "lost" ones to make decisions. Reminding a child that he is the "only one left who is not baptized" puts undue pressure on a child. He feels forced to make a profession of faith to keep from failing in the eyes of someone he respects. Is such a motive worthy?

There are those, too, who play a numbers game with our children. Some evangelists and pastors will use pressure tactics to get people down the aisle. Children, of course, are very susceptible to such pressure or methods. The motive of such people seems to be to get a large response. I believe in a large response to the preaching of the gospel, but I do not believe in response at any price. Some preachers, however, will misuse the invitation time or their own personal position to embarrass, scare, or manipulate people down the aisles. Such can be the source of frustrations and later doubts for children as they try to understand if they truly responded for themselves or if they responded to the pressure of the moment.

There are nationally known organizations which are

seeking the conversion of our children. One should examine such organizations before he allows his children to become involved with them. A reading of their correspondence materials and a talk with a director in your area may help you to understand their philosophy and methods in childhood conversion. You may find some things acceptable while you may question others. For example, you may raise your eyebrows when you learn that one organization trains telephone counselors to talk with children about being saved. They may call a home and talk to a child whom they have never seen before. There is no personal contact other than the phone conversation. Yet, the assumption is that this counselor has the right to talk to a child about being saved.

Questions to Ask

There are several questions which will help you focus on the issues which have been presented in the preceding pages. These questions may be asked of yourself, the worker with children, pastor, evangelist, or organizational representative.

1. Is this person genuinely concerned about my child? What proof is there of such interest apart from this effort to convert him?

2. What is this person's view of evangelism? Evangelism involves more than getting people saved. It means caring for and nurturing them once the decision for Christ has been made. Is this person interested in my child's further spiritual growth? In what ways?

3. Is the methodology used by this person consistent with the work of the Holy Spirit? Only God's Spirit can

bring about conversion. Only the Spirit can make a person truly willing to receive Jesus. Some tactics which pressure and manipulate people usurp the power which belongs only to God.

4. Does this person share with you, the parent, the conversation or methods used with the child?

II
Important Issues
in Religious Training

6

Values and Conversion

A young woman was baking a cake for a friend. While attempting to blend the ingredients into a unified mixture, she was interrupted by the telephone, doorbell, and her child wanting attention. After each interruption, she proceeded to prepare the mixture for baking. About the time the young woman placed the mixture into the oven for baking, she discovered that she had failed to add the two cups of sugar called for in the recipe. She responded by emptying the ingredients into the mixing bowl again and stirring in the sugar in the hope that it would blend properly at this stage.

Developing values in children is sometimes approached the same way by parents. They realize, almost too late, that something important has been left out and try to blend it into the child's life at the last moment. The problem with such an approach is that developing values is not so simple as blending ingredients to bake a cake.

What are the factors which converge upon a child's life to influence the development of his values and, thus, his choice concerning Jesus as Savior? This chapter will briefly discuss these factors.

The Role of Values

There is the sneaking suspicion by most parents that the ideas, habits, and ideals to which children are exposed do affect them. Parents often do not understand what those factors are and how they influence the child. The child is not simply the product of all the things he has seen, heard, smelled, touched, and tasted. Rather, he is a product of an interpretation of his experiences—an interpretation based upon what is important and what is not important in life. Thus, the influences which converge upon a child's life are interpreted through a set of values which are developing in the child. The influence a person or idea will have upon the child's life depends upon how the child responds to the person or idea.

The Importance of Values

Before proceeding to a discussion of the factors involved in the development of values, we should attempt to determine what is meant by the term *value*. We should ask: "What is the role of values?" Also we should clarify the relationship between a child's values and his choice of Jesus as Savior.

What Are Values?

To value something is to place worth upon it. A child may value a toy, a game, the television, parents, or friends. Values are attitudes about the importance of certain things in life. Values, then, are relative or have a gradation according to the object to which worth is being ascribed. Hopefully, parents can guide their children to place great importance upon that which is most worthy and less value on those things which are less important.

All persons have values. The question is: What do they value most, and are those things which they value worthy of the importance given to them?

Values and Choices

There is a positive relationship between that which a person values and the choices he makes. For instance, in a situation in which you would have to choose to betray a friend or to advance yourself, your values would be the determining factor in your choice. While alternatives are not always so easy to decide, values play an important role in the choices you make. Jesus was very clear about the relationship of values and choices. Matthew records the following statements: "Where your treasure is, there will your heart be also"(6:21). "Out of the heart come evil thoughts, murder, adultery, fornication, theft, false witness, slander"(15:19).

A child's choice concerning Jesus as Savior is directly related to how he values Jesus and what Jesus offers to those who trust Him. It is important for the child to be able to respond from a background which has clearly emphasized Christian values.

Factors Influencing Value Development

There are several influences which converge upon a child's life which seek to mold the structure of his value system and, thus, his life. These influences could be identified according to three broad categories: family, religion, and society.

Family and Values

The family relationship, more than any other, is the basic influence on the value development of children. For good or bad children learn their basic attitudes and develop a system for judging the worth of people and things from the family. Oscar Feucht, writing in *Family Relationships and the Church* (St. Louis: Concordia, 1971, p. 7) has correctly stated, "The moral and spiritual images which children develop come largely from values lived in the home."

It would be difficult to underestimate the amount a child learns through his family. Feucht said in *Helping Families Through the Church* (St. Louis: Concordia, 1971, p. 63), "The home is potentially the greatest teacher." Think of some ways in which this is true.

A child learns prejudice or love through his home. He learns to be appreciative or ungrateful the same way. His basic outlook on the purpose of life, the person of Jesus, and the worth of self and others is formulated primarily in relationship to home, particularly his parents.

Consistency is the key to teaching values to your child. If your example complements your words, your child will find security in believing in what you are and say. Inconsistency, to the contrary, will cause confusion, doubt, and cynicism. Obviously, who a parent is and what he does is a very weighty matter in the teaching of values to his children.

One of the most alarming aspects of teaching values relates to the young child's lack of discrimination. He does not know a good example from a bad one. He tends to model his parent without stopping to ask about the moral consequences. His trust is so complete and so naive that whatever the parent does is acceptable. Such an awareness on the part of the parent must have given birth to the following poem by an unknown author.

A careful man I want to be,
A little fellow follows me,
I do not dare to go astray,
For fear he'll go the selfsame way.

I cannot once escape his eyes,
Whate'er he sees me do, he tries,
Like me he says he's going to be,
The little chap who follows me.

He thinks that I am good and fine,
Believes in every word of mine,
The base in me, he must not see,
The little chap who follows me.

I must remember as I go,
Through summer's sun, and winter's snow,
I am building for the years to be,
That little chap who follows me.

Religion and Values

Another great force influencing the development of a child's values is religion. Religious instruction, whether at home or at church, is based upon the value system of the particular denomination or faith. It is the goal of each religious group for its members to follow certain values or live according to its teachings.

The Christian faith is based upon values found in the statement made in Luke 10:27: "You shall love the Lord your God with all your heart, and with all your soul, and with all your strength, and with all your mind; and your neighbor as yourself." Jesus expressed the foundational values of Christianity in similar words: "You shall love the Lord your God with all your heart, and with all your soul, and with all your mind. This is the great and first commandment. And a second is like it, You shall love your neighbor as yourself. On these two commandments depend all the law and the prophets" (Matt. 22:37-40).

An analysis of these passages will readily reveal that the Christian religion and all its corresponding values is based upon values related to three major areas. One must have a proper love for God, self, and others. One must love God supremely. One must love other people as oneself. This implies a proper love or respect for one's own life or personhood.

The home and church should work together to teach religious values to children. They are partners, not competitors, in this venture. The church is the center of formal instruction. There are structured classes with the goal of teaching certain values. The Sunday School, training sessions, mission activities, and music activities should all strive to teach the basics of the faith and to train children how to apply these values to life.

The home is the informal center for teaching values. While there may be such structured religious instruction as family devotions and prayer at meals, the home, and its involvements, is a prime setting for value development. Values related to God, Jesus, Bible, self, and others can be related in ways which will leave lasting impressions.

Children who are taught Christian values in a consistent manner will become sensitive to their inability to live up to such values. This allows the possibility to recognize oneself as a sinner or lawbreaker. The Holy Spirit uses such feelings of moral inadequacy and guilt to direct the child to Jesus as Savior. This is not a forced or contrived matter, but it is a relationship with parents and Christian workers where the Holy Spirit is allowed to work through the witness of their lives to bring the child to Jesus. How wonderful it is for the child to come to the point of conversion realizing that parents, teachers, and leaders have nurtured him and love him.

Society and Values

One almost becomes paranoid on realizing all the influences outside the home and church which converge upon a child's life. While there are many good influences, we as parents tend to think in terms of the challenges negative influences present to our child's value system.

What are some of the most obvious and powerful societal factors? Television is certainly a factor which must be reckoned with. One cannot help but believe that children who are constantly bombarded with the violence, sexual looseness, and general disrespect for life and property seen on many television programs will soon begin to incorporate such ideas into their values system. Parents should work through national organizations to change such influences. They can also be discriminate about what their children watch on television. Also, parents can turn the television off if there is nothing appropriate for viewing.

Mobility in our society also affects the values of our

children. Some children move every few years and may soon lose a feeling of permanence or the need to make friends. This constant mobility will likely bring children into contact with others who have a radically different view of God and the values of the Christian faith. While we cannot protect our children from such diversity, we must be aware that it exists and can cause value confusion in our children. We must constantly reinforce the values of our faith to counteract this confusion.

Materialism is a philosophy of life which has infiltrated almost every facet of our existence. Children of this day are constantly bombarded by "things." They have more things than any past generation. The danger is in placing too much value on possessions and in building one's values on something which is not permanent. An outgrowth of this philosophy is using people to gain possessions. This is clearly a violation of the Christian value system. In order to counteract this philosophy, parents must keep the relationship of persons and things in proper perspective. Possessions or material things were made to serve people and not vice versa.

Another influence on the values of children is the peer group. Children between 6 and 12 years of age tend to group themselves with friends of the same age and same sex. These groups or clubs have their own language and attitudes which have not been taught at home. While these may cause concern for a parent, they are temporary deviations which can be overcome with patience and a consistent, understanding home environment. Perhaps one of the greatest dangers of peer influence is for one child to "walk the aisle" because he has seen a friend do it and feels it would cause him to be accepted if he did like-wise. A child's need to be accepted by age-mates is a powerful influence and should be examined by the parents if there is suspicion that such is involved in their child's decision to accept Jesus as Savior.

This section on societal influences on values has been limited in its approach, but it does show in a small way how some of the major influences operate to influence parent and child and the implications of these influences for value development.

7

Discerning the Signs

Most parents recognize that timing is important in rearing children. Educator Robert Havighurst has referred to the most opportune time for teaching and learning as the "teachable moment." Havighurst believes that there is a period when a child is socially and mentally ready to learn. Certain social and mental conditions have to be right before a child is at a peak time for learning, for example, such things as math concepts. Until the child is ready to learn, maximum effort at teaching brings only minimum results in learning.

Yes, timing is important in rearing children. Sometimes we wrongly assume that there is a certain age when we must teach our child about such things as sex and other subjects necessary for their proper adjustment. The pitfall to this kind of approach is well illustrated in this humorous incident. The father of an eleven-year-old was told by his wife that it was time for him to sit down and talk with their son about sex. The father managed to muster up the courage to face the issue. He decided that the

next Saturday morning was the proper time to thorough-
ly explain the facts with a carefully prepared talk. Saturday arrived, and the father proceeded with his well-de-
vised plan. Sitting on the side of his son's bed the father
talked. The boy listened intently for an hour or more.
Quite proud that the talk had gone so smoothly, the father closed by asking, "Now, Son, do you have any questions you want to ask me?" "Just one," the boy replied.
"Can I go outside and play now?"

Indeed, timing is important in rearing children. This is
true in all phases of their growing and learning. Knowing
when your child is ready to respond to Christ as Savior is
the first step in assuring helpful guidance on your part.

When Is a Child Ready?

The answer to this question will vary from child to
child. This is true even in a family where children have
been reared under quite similar conditions. Children
themselves are different and grow and develop at different rates. Age does not really enter the picture in the
sense that we can set a definite chronological point at
which all children are capable of trusting Christ as Savior. Some children may be capable of a valid decision by a
young age. Others may be an older age before they are
capable of such a decision.

This is a perplexing problem for parents. How much
easier it would be if there were a uniform age at which all
children should become Christians. This, however, is not
the case, and parents are left to agonize over this problem
of determining when their children are ready.

Many parents are reluctant to allow their children to

make a public commitment to Christ because of a bad experience of being pushed into something themselves or being restrained from a public decision by their parents. We do not want to push our children to make a decision which they will later feel was not meaningful to them. Yet, we do not want them to delay making their decision for Christ once they are ready. We must be sure that we neither restrain nor push a child. child can make a valid decision to trust Christ once she realizes she has sinned against God and need to trust Christ as her Savior. How do we determine when our children have reached that point?

The Stirring of the Spirit

One of the wonderful mysteries of life is the way the Spirit of God works in people's lives to bring them to faith in Christ. Prior to Christian conversion, the Holy Spirit's work is that of creating a sense of need in the unbeliever by revealing two things. First, the person is led to see himself as a sinner, helpless, and in need. Next, he is led to see that Christ is the Savior of sinners and is pure and lovely, all that the sinner is not. By creating this tension or guilt over the sinner's relationship to God, the Holy Spirit purposes to bring the person to a place where he will turn from his sin and to Christ as Savior in repentance and faith. This experience is usually an uncomfortable one, even for a child. The stirring of the Spirit in a child's life may be manifested in one or a combination of several ways.

Change in Behavior

Children have patterns of behavior which are quite

normal for them. We can usually predict how they will act or react in a familiar situation. We may know, for example, that Jennie is afraid of dogs and will show her fear while Tommy will react favorably to the presence of a dog. Awareness of their behavior patterns can help us understand and guide them when they need our help.

A child who is being dealt with by the Holy Spirit will usually show changes in behavior. Moodiness or irritability may be the sign of the Spirit's work. Behavior change may be especially noticeable in a child who is usually quiet. If the child becomes loud and aggressive, something is happening. Conversely, a loud and active child might become quiet and less energetic. This, too, may indicate something deep and troubling.

While changes in the activity level are caused by various things, such as sickness or death, it is well for you to be aware that conviction of sin may also show similar symptoms. Do not automatically assume that a change in behavior is caused by any one thing. Stay in touch with what is happening with your child so that you can be sensitive at all times, especially when there is the stirring of the Spirit in her life.

Questions

Nothing serves to keep a parent on mental tiptoes like fielding questions from a child. Life overflows with mystery and wonder; the child is curious to know all, and more, that his parents can tell him. Asking questions is a natural avenue of learning for a child and should be accepted as such by the parent. The seemingly endless barrage of questions is not an attempt to test your patience but to arrive at a satisfying answer.

Children ask questions about almost everything, including religion. How do you handle those questions and determine where a child is spiritually?

Religious questions do not indicate necessarily that a child is ready to accept Christ as Savior. Questions, however, do mark the beginning of the child's search for religious truth. You should cultivate this interest by being alert to their searching and by honestly attempting to answer their questions.

Questions may often indicate that a child feels a need to conform to what she sees others do. For instance, a parent should not automatically interpret the question: When can I get baptized? to mean that the child is ready to receive Christ as Savior. You may discover that the child sees baptism as a means of conforming to what others in her group are doing. Such questions as: When can I go forward and accept Christ as my Savior? seems to indicate more concern for the need of salvation than does the former one.

Here are some important guidelines about answering your child's questions. These suggestions are generally applicable to any area in which your child may question.

Treat every question as important. Do not minimize the significance of your child's questions. If you answer the simple ones, you will likely be asked to help with those which are really troublesome. Remember that curiosity is one of a child's best ways of learning and that questions are an expression of that curiosity.

Understand the question your child is asking. One of the serious problems of handling children's questions can be resolved if we seek to determine *what* the child is attempting to ask. Parents often assume that a child is asking about something which does not yet concern her. Before answering, it is a good thing to ask yourself, What does she want to know?

Answer the question simply and briefly. We should be courteous enough to answer only the question a child asks. We should not use the occasion of one question as an opportunity for a discourse on God's entire plan of salvation. If we overload the child with facts and concepts, we will confuse rather than simplify the matter for him. The child will likely hesitate to ask again if we insist on telling him more than he wants to know or is able to receive at this time. Keep your answers brief and simple.

Ask her to explain in her own words. We can clarify much for a child if we will ask her to tell us why she asks a certain question. After we have attempted to answer the question, it might be well for us to ask:" Did that answer your question?" If you have been on target you might pursue beyond that question to the reason for the question:" Would you like to tell me, in your own words, why you have asked me this question?" Listen carefully. Your child's reply could indicate the depth of her spiritual understanding.

Change in Interest Level

Another possible sign of conviction is your child's change in interest regarding religious things. For instance, your child might suddenly become enthralled with Sunday School and Bible study. He might begin to listen very intently to what the pastor is saying, especially at the time of the invitation. This sudden interest may be directly related to the stirring of the Spirit in his life.

There is also the possibility of the opposite reactions to that just described. A child who has been attending Sunday School and church regularly may suddenly become ill and wish not to attend. A child may invent a thousand ways to excuse herself from the worship service because she must face the issue of her sins during the invitation period. Be aware that this sudden shift in interest may be an attempt to escape the conviction work of the Holy Spirit in her life. Above all, be understanding and encourage your child to share with you why there has been this change in her interest regarding Bible study and worship.

Conclusion

Recognizing the possible signs of conviction is an important step in helping your child express his faith in Christ as Savior. Hopefully, the foregoing suggestions and clues will help you "tune in" to your child when he asks you to guide him on his spiritual pilgrimage.

8
Talking Religion

Advertisers spend billions of dollars annually to communicate the benefits of their product to the public. We are constantly reminded of how vitally such companies believe in communication by billboards, newspapers and magazines, television and radio, and a variety of other ways advertisers attempt to get their messages to us.

Communication is the giving and receiving of information. Such a process is vitally important in the proper functioning of the home. This is especially true for Christian parents who are attempting to guide their children in the quest for the truth concerning God and His plan for their lives.

Here are some suggestions which, if followed, will help to keep the lines of communication open between parents and children. First, make all subjects open for discussion. Some children do not feel at ease talking about God because He is never a part of normal conversation in the home. Parents, by their willingness to respond to all and any questions, can help their children know that all subjects can be discussed. Second, the parents' example must complement their teaching. Many parents find that the spiritual pilgrimage of their children sensitizes them to the inadequacies of their own lives. There is for some that nagging, gnawing awareness of the inconsistencies which exist between what they say and what they do. Communication about God tends to break down when the child realizes that what parents are talking about is not really so important to the parents. Third, we must attempt to be good listeners. Listening shows that we are really interested in what the child is saying. Listening communicates concern and enhances the possibility of further conversation.

Now let's look at some specific problems related to talking religion with a child.

Religious Words

Words are the primary units of speech by which we communicate with each other. A word can have many different meanings depending on the context or the way in which it is combined with other words.

Religious subjects are generally more difficult to talk about because many terms we use have special religious meanings. Often these terms mean something else when used in conversation not primarily of a religious nature. The "language of Zion" can often hinder communication. As adults, we use such words as *saved, lost, salvation, faith, redemption, repent, love, heaven,* and *hell* with some degree of understanding of their meanings. But few children understand the religious meanings of such words unless we take the time to explain.

Imagine how confusing religious jargon can be to the child who does not understand it. Suppose you suspect that your child is expressing some sign of conviction. With great concern you ask him such questions as: "Do

you feel that you are under conviction for your sins? Do
you feel that you are lost?"

There are at least three words in these questions which
may confuse the child. What are they? *Conviction* is a le-
gal term. *Sin* is a moral term. *Lost* is generally used in
terms of geographical location. Take a moment to think
how you could substitute a word for each of these which
would help to simplify communication.

Have you ever wished that a doctor, lawyer, or dentist
would talk in terms that you could understand? Have you
ever left their offices not knowing what was said or what
you were to do? This is the same type of confusion children face when we assume that they will understand
what we intend to communicate by religious words. Just
because they nod approval of what we say does not mean
that they understand.

One helpful solution to this problem is to translate religious terminology into language a child can understand.
This will cause many fretful moments for you but the results will be worth it. Why talk to your child about religion if he cannot understand what you are saying?

Here is a brief list of words which we often use in religious talk. What is the meaning of each of them, and what
is a good, simple way of saying the same thing?

sin	heart
faith	baptize
repent	church
salvation	church member
sanctification	conviction

Now, let's look at some ways of explaining these words
so your child can understand them.

Sin. Sin is when you do something wrong against God.

It is when you choose to do what you want to do when God wants you to do something else.

Faith. Faith is when you trust God to do what He says He will do. It is to do what God says because you believe that is the best thing to do.

Repent. When you decide that you will no longer continue to do a certain thing because it is wrong, you repent. You are sorry for what you did against God and don't want to ever do it again.

Salvation. Salvation is when God forgives your wrongs against Him because you have told Him you were sorry for not believing in Him. Now you are willing to trust Him and do what He wants you to do.

Sanctification. This is something like what happens to your body. When you are a baby, you need to grow up to be an adult. Sanctification is a growth process of your attitudes where you grow more and more to be loving and kind like Jesus.

Heart. Heart, in this case, is the part of us which causes us to act in good or bad ways. In our heart we believe some things are very important while others are not very important. We make choices based on what we believe, in our heart, is important. When Jesus comes to live in our life, he wants to change our heart so we can act in ways that please him. He helps us understand and do what is best.

Baptize. When people who have trusted Jesus to forgive their wrongs against Him are put under the water by the pastor to show others that Jesus has forgiven them, they are baptized.

Church. A church is a group of people who believe in Jesus as the One who forgives them. They meet in a church building or some other place to learn about Him, ways to do good for others, and tell others about Him.

Church Member. A church member is a person who has joined with others who believe in Jesus in order to learn more about Him, to do good for others, and to tell others about Him.

Conviction. When a people feel guilty or troubled over something they have done wrong against God, we say they are under conviction. It is a feeling of failure to do what God wanted and that one is unable to do what God wants without His help.

Literal Vs. Symbolic Language

Another area of concern in in religious conversation with children is their tendency to make literal interpretations of what we say. While there are some exceptions to the rule, children generally do not understand symbolic language.

The ever-present danger of this, of course, is for a child to take as literal something which we mean symbolically. For instance, someone may tell the child to "let Jesus come into your heart." The symbolic idea is an excellent one, but one which, when couched in such language, may cause some real problems for the literal-minded child.

Another example of how symbolic language may confuse the child is the word *lost*. The child may have lost a nickel or a favorite toy. He can understand the literal significance of that term. But can he really be expected to appreciate the spiritual meaning which is symbolized? If you ask the child if he is lost, he may just stare at you. Or again he may say, "No, but my toy is lost."

Such phrases as "washed in the blood" can also cause

some real problems in interpretation for a child. Can you imagine what fantastic and gory images a child could conjure up by taking such a phrase at face value!

Caution also needs to be used in explaining the meaning of symbols, such as baptism and the Lord's Supper. It is not uncommon for a child to believe that baptism washes a person's sins away. Likewise, many children believe that the Lord's Supper is a literal eating of Jesus' body and drinking of His blood. These are beautiful ordinances in their symbolic meanings but fall short of their true value when approached literally.

Whenever possible, such symbolic language should be avoided in favor of language which is more easily understood. Whenever we cannot avoid symbols, we should make sure that our child understands their meanings.

Abstract Vs. Concrete

There are several ideas or concepts in Christianity which are difficult for a child to understand. They are also difficult for adults to understand. Parents need to be aware of some of these areas in order to give the child a clearer understanding of the basic teachings of the Christian faith.

Something abstract cannot be thought of or adequately described in purely physical or material terms. The child is basically concrete in his understanding of concepts and ideas.

Many Christian concepts are abstract. The child basically interprets them in a concrete way. For example, he will normally think of the church as a physical building rather than as a body of baptized believers. He is also likely to think of God as a big man with human features. The concept of the Holy Spirit as God really baffles him, especially when he attempts to visualize the Spirit in concrete form.

Here are some things to keep in mind as you talk to your child about God.

First, accept the fact that your child thinks in concrete terms. Your attempts to communicate should not degrade God and the Holy Spirit to human status. However, you should select terms which accurately tell some of the truth you understand. God is the Creator, Maker of all the world. A child can appreciate this truth because he can relate God to the physical world. At the same time you are able to speak of an idea that is awe-inspiring to the child.

Second, correct understanding of theology is not necessary for salvation. One must understand who Jesus is and what is necessary to receive Him as Savior, but one's salvation is not determined by how much factual knowledge or spiritual discernment one has.

Third, God is the revealer of the deep mysteries of salvation to the child. The Holy Spirit is working in his life long before he can either understand or explain Him. As a parent, you may serve as God's instrument to help your child, but only God can give understanding of His truth. Depend on this, and your worry and anxiety will decrease.

Fourth, talk to your child mainly in terms of Jesus. Children relate easily to Jesus because they can visualize Him and can listen to stories about Him. If children can understand the love and character of Jesus, they can understand the basic nature of the Father and the Holy Spirit.

Fifth, accept the fact that many things must wait until the child is older and can understand better. There will be time later for him to grapple with some of the deep, abstract concepts of the Christian faith.

Let Him Explain

One of the easiest errors to commit while talking about religion with children is to make statements or to ask questions which anticipate a simple, positive response. The main problem with this kind of questioning is that it does not give the child an opportunity to explain his concern. We should avoid questions which are designed to get the child to answer yes or no. Obviously, we can make a "Christian" out of any child by simply asking the right questions and getting the right answer.

Part of the problem is that children are prone to want to say what they think we want to hear. A better approach is to ask questions which will require a thoughtful answer. We should not allow our anxiety or concern to see our child converted push us to formulate a statement of faith to which he must only give an affirmative answer.

Allowing the child to express his own thoughts and feelings has advantages. This helps you understand the level of his thinking, and it helps him clarify what she really does believe at this stage.

Questions or statements which make the child think are most effective. For example, a question such as: Why do you think you need to become a Christian? can expose many of the child's thoughts and feelings. Remember that questions with why, what, or how at the front of them are most likely to provide the real reasons and ideas you need to hear.

9

The Gospel for Children

During the invitation in a Sunday morning worship service which I had led, Denise, an eight-year-old girl, stepped into the aisle and came forward. As I greeted her, I asked, "Why have you come?" As I bent to her level, she whispered, "To say that I love Jesus."

Denise was not received for church membership and baptism that day. A brief period of counseling following the service proved that such an action would have been premature. Her response to several questions revealed that her grasp of basic facts of the gospel was inadequate for a genuine profession of faith.

It is admirable for us to teach our children to say, "I love Jesus" or to sing "Jesus loves me." But their ability to do so does not indicate that they are ready to receive Jesus as Savior.

One Gospel for All?

Denise needed time to grow in her understanding of some fundamental gospel concepts before she would be able to respond in repentance and faith in Christ. To have accepted her for baptism and church membership would have harmed her spiritually. Such a procedure would also have violated a personal conviction that there is one gospel for all—adults and children alike.

Yes, there is but one gospel. The basic facts of this gospel must be accepted by all, children included, before one can receive forgiveness of sins. We make a grave error when we attempt to usher children into the kingdom when they do not know the King or what He requires for citizenship in His kingdom.

Perhaps we should be reminded that our God is one who deals in mercy and compassion toward His people. We can take comfort in knowing that God does not hold our children responsible for sin until they are able to respond to the basic facts of the gospel.

Head Knowledge and the Holy Spirit

If we assume that the acceptance of certain facts is essential for salvation, we must concede that such facts are somehow gained through the intellectual process. This means that a child must first be introduced to these facts in some manner, such as through a Bible story or sermon. (Read Rom. 10:8-10.) Another implication is that children will understand at different levels, according to their experience and intelligence.

Particular caution should be stressed at this point concerning what true understanding of the gospel is. Head knowledge is absolutely essential but is inadequate to save. The Holy Spirit is the convicting and saving agent. He alone brings true understanding. The Spirit's role is to work with the facts and experiences of the person (the child) to bring about a sense of need and a response to the

Savior. The Holy Spirit applies the basic facts of the gospel to the spiritual life of the child, thus making the gospel more than just a set of memorized facts. Under the teaching of the Spirit, the child comes to understand sin, the cross, and the resurrection as having intensely personal meanings.

The Gospel

The gospel, or good news about Jesus, is for children too. There are some ideas basic to, and connected with, God's plan of salvation which persons must understand before they can trust Christ as Savior. What are the basics of the gospel? There are four interrelated areas.

1. Jesus is the Savior sent from God. Recognition of the person and the mission of Jesus is obviously necessary to salvation. He is not just a good man or just a prophet but the Son of God who came to save us from our sins. He is the One through whom we must come to God. Note such passages as Matthew 1:21; 16:16; and Luke 19:10 for clear biblical statements of this fact.

2. Personal sin separates us from God. The child who does not recognize the problem of personal sin in his life is not ready to respond to Christ as Savior. The person who sincerely seeks to know Jesus as Savior has first realized a need or lack in his life which only Jesus can meet. He has seen himself as one guilty of breaking God's law. There is a sense of guilt concerning sin and a desperate or inadequate feeling about dealing with the problem alone. There is an awareness of separation from God which can only be remedied when a right relationship to God is restored. Verses such as Romans 3:23 and 6:23 relate to this area of need.

3. What Christ did provides forgiveness of sins. What did Christ do to forgive our sins? Two things. First, He bore the guilt of our sins and died for them on the cross. He died in our place. He took our sins upon Himself. He took the penalty of sin (death) on the cross. Second, He arose from the dead on the third day to prove that He has power over sin and can really forgive us. The resurrection is the proof that His death on the cross really provides forgiveness for those who believe.

4. Repentance and faith are necessary to receive forgiveness of sin. Repentance is an attitude of mind in which a person willfully turns away from sin. Repentance means renouncing sin as a way of living. Saving faith is a turning to Christ, trusting Him to forgive our sin and to bring us into a right relationship with God. Repentance and faith are complementary attitudes of the will by which life's direction is changed.

Forgiveness of sin necessitates a response on the part of the individual. By their own choosing, persons must turn from sin and commit themselves to Christ and His way of life.

One word of caution is necessary concerning the child and the gospel. We should not impose adult standards of understanding upon a child. While he should have a clear grasp of the basic facts, he should not be expected to express his faith in adult terms or thoughts. To expect a child to give a clearly defined theology of salvation is to demand more than most children and adults are capable of doing. The child does not understand or respond on the adult level. God honors a child's faith, based on a child's limited understanding of the basics of the gospel.

The Person of the Gospel

We must ever keep in mind that the heart of the Christian gospel is not a certain formula to which all the saved must subscribe but a living person—Jesus Christ. Do not minimize a child's ability to perceive the spiritual realities necessary to respond positively to Jesus. We should remember that Jesus used a child as the standard of measurement for those who would enter His kingdom (Mark 10:13-16).

It is our task to teach the facts about this Person to our children and to be a living example of His power. The Holy Spirit will then make real the Person of Jesus in the lives of our children.

Points to Ponder

The following ideas were stressed in this chapter.

1. There is one gospel for adults and children alike. We should not decrease the demands of the gospel for children.

2. Understanding of certain facts of the gospel is absolutely necessary before a child can believe. The Holy Spirit applies these learned facts to bring about conversion.

3. There are four interrelated areas of the gospel about which a child should have a clear understanding. These areas relate to the Person and work of Jesus and the problem of sin and its solution.

4. Children should not be expected to understand at adult levels. To demand such is to substitute the ability to understand and to communicate for faith.

5. While certain beliefs are necessary, Christianity is a relationship to the Person of Jesus Christ. We should teach the basic facts and allow the Holy Spirit to make the Person of the gospel real to our children.

III
Teaching the Faith

Introduction

Before proceeding to the strategies on the following pages, it would be well to think about some suggestions related to those strategies but not necessarily included in the chapters which follow. This overview is intended to give you an introduction to the subject areas, procedures, and methods which you may use in discussing conversion and the basics of the Christian faith with a child.

A quick glance at the chapters included in this section will show that seven subject areas are discussed. These chapters are arranged in a progressive sequence, but individual chapters can be utilized with children who are already past the initial stage and are experiencing concern at another point, such as prayer or baptism. The entire section can be used as a good review for children who have already had a conversion experience.

Each chapter is designed with a definite, stated objective, suggested procedure, and methodology. Be certain that you clearly understand the objective or aim before proceeding. Procedures and methods are matched to the chapter objective but may be altered to fit your particular resources or time schedule. Feel free to make adaptations as long as you keep the objective in view. Methods must serve to fulfill the aim or else they can become an obstacle to it.

The chapters are designed to be covered in one session each. The final chapter is not intended for a conference situation with children, thus six sessions will be required. Most of the subjects covered will require 30 minutes to an hour or longer, depending upon the amount of questions or discussion. Be sure the child understands each step before proceeding to the next. For this reason, it may be well to cover the same subject two or more times.

The design of this section is for a more formal type of home teaching. It will have best results when there are definite periods of time set aside. Perhaps this can be done over a week, two weeks, or a month. One parent or both parents can be involved, according to the needs of other family members. It is suggested, however, that this not be done with parents alternating the responsibility, since both parents may not be aware of what was said or specifically related in the previous session.

We should remember that the most effective learning takes place when the child is ready to learn. Pay close attention to your child and do not force him into these sessions if he has no interest in becoming a Christian at this point. A brief review of the chapter "Discerning the Signs" will be helpful at the point of knowing when he is ready for such an involvement.

You will notice upon further investigation that each chapter is designed in a child-centered fashion. The leader becomes a guide in the activities as the child's ideas and understanding are called forth.

As you read each chapter, do so with the prayer that God will lead you to a deeper understanding of your child and the relevance of this material for her life. Pause often to reflect on the suggestions which are made. Do you understand them? If not, read them until you do.

One problem you may encounter in applying some methods and concepts with your child is that the methods and concepts may not correspond with your child's level of development. Children follow certain developmental patterns, and each child has his own rate of progress within the pattern. Be sensitive to your child's level of understanding and adapt the materials to his needs. Read each session with your child in mind and plan for the changes which your child's level of understanding will dictate.

10

God, the Loving Creator

How do you understand if a child really believes? That is, how do you know the difference between "saying words" and knowledge revealed to the child by the Holy Spirit? This is a perplexing problem to anyone who has talked with a child about trusting Jesus as Savior. Words are easy to say but do not always reveal the depth of a person's commitment to Jesus. The ability to say "I love Jesus" or "I want Jesus to come into my heart" does not mean that a child is ready to become a Christian. Further investigation needs to be made to determine what the child means or just why he has made such a statement.

Session Objectives

This chapter attempts to assist parents in determining whether their child is ready to trust Jesus and to help them guide their child in this time of commitment to Jesus. More specifically, the chapter objectives are:

1. To help parents identify where their child is in relationship to trusting Jesus as Savior.

2. To involve the child in learning activities which will help her understand what is involved in trusting Jesus as Savior.

Major Concepts

This session is designed with four major, interrelated concepts. There is such a progression of thought that the flow of one area into the next should seem quite natural. The major concepts are: (1) God, the loving Creator, (2) the problem of sin, (3) God's solution for our problem, and (4) repentance, faith, and forgiveness.

Resources

The following materials are needed for this session.

Pictures. These pictures may be cut from various types of magazines and each pasted separately on a piece of attractive construction paper. Suggested pictures of creation are: animals, trees, clouds, flowers, sun, moon, man and woman, Jesus.

Words. Sin, repent, and life. Print each word in bold letters on a 3 by 5 card or piece of paper.

Other. A blank piece of paper or chalkboard will be needed for writing.

Bible. A version which the child can read easily will be best.

Procedure

The purpose in discussing God, the loving Creator, is to begin with an idea the child can readily understand. A child first understands God as Creator, then later as Savior. The concept of loving Creator is discussed in order to show God's love and to set the background for understanding the nature of sin and God's provision for those who turn to Him in trust. The Bible background for this concept is the first three chapters of Genesis.

With your Bible open to Genesis 1 for reference purposes, begin the discussion on God, the loving Creator. A good way to begin is to spread the creation pictures before the child and ask her to pick out two or three to talk about. Ask her to respond to this question concerning each picture which she chose: What does this picture tell you about God? Guide your child to understand that God made everything with purpose and order and in loving concern for human beings.

Next, take the creation pictures and go through the order of creation, stressing some of the purposes the object in each picture may serve. For example, you may tell how God made clouds to give rain for things upon earth to grow. This shows God's care. The climax to this sequence should be brought into focus for the child by asking: But why did God make all of these things? What was the last and most important thing He made? Allow comments or answers and show the picture of people as God's creation. Emphasize that God made everything for our good and enjoyment. God made people to be partners in caring for all created things. This tells us that God loves human beings more than anything else He has made. More than the sun, stars, trees, or animals.

In order for people to be happy, God gave them some rules or laws to live by. Ask: Do you know what happened? How did the man and women act toward this loving Creator who had made everything for their good? Allow the child to express answers about how Adam and Eve broke God's rules. Hold up the card with the word *sin* written on it. Ask, Do you know what this word means? Allow your child to express her ideas. Listen closely to her concept of sin. Sin is more than doing wrong. It is more than disobeying Mother and Daddy. It is more than doing something and getting caught. Help your child see that Adam and Eve sinned by disobeying God, who was good and loving to them. Sin is against God. It is the doing of what God forbids and the unwillingness to do what God tells us to do. Help your child understand that behind all different kinds of sins is the sin of doing things your own way and not trusting Jesus.

Ask: Do you have sins? If your child answers no, then obviously she does not sense her guilt. If the answer is yes, then ask your child to share with you what some of her sins are. Open your Bible to Exodus 20 to the Ten Commandments and help your child see how her sins are the breaking of God's rules for life. You may expect to hear answers of everyday types of sins, such as lying and stealing. Do not pass over these as nothing. If your child speaks of such as sin, apparently the Holy Spirit has convicted her of such.

If your child senses such guilt for her moral shortcomings, then she is guilty before God. She needs to be led to see something of her situation before God. Lead her to read Romans 3:23 and Romans 6:23 from the Bible. Romans 3:23 tells him that she, like all other persons, has sinned against a loving God who made her. To "fall short of the glory of God" means that God has a high standard for us to live by (His laws), and we have all failed to meet that standard. Romans 6:23 tells of the result of sin and the provision God has made because we are sinners. The "wages of sin" may need to be explained in terms of payment received for doing something. The payment we get for sinning against God is death—eternal separation from God beginning the moment we sin. We feel guilty for our sins and are out of God's presence because of our sins. You may want to illustrate this in the story of Adam and Eve in Genesis 3:8,23-24.

God cares so much for us that He seeks to help us even when we break His laws and sin against Him. Ask, What did He do to bring us back into His presence and to take away our guilt? Allow an answer. Show the picture of Jesus. Have your child read or quote John 3:16 and tell you again what God has done. Ask: Why did God send Jesus? Why did Jesus die for us? *(To take the penalty or payment for our sins.)* Emphasize that Jesus came to love us and to bring us back to God. He came to be our Savior from sin. But we must all accept God's gift of Jesus for ourselves. In Romans 6:23 God tells us there are two ways to live. We can take the payment for our sins, or we can accept His gift of life in Jesus. This gift is only in Jesus.

Illustrate how one must receive Jesus in order to receive the life He gives. Place the word *life* in your Bible and say, How can you get this card with the word *life* written on it? *(By first taking the Bible in which it is placed.)* Likewise the life which God gives is in Jesus, and one must receive Him in order to have life. At this point, ask your child if she understands how Jesus gives us life and if she wants to accept Him as her Savior. Spend as much time as needed in clarifying and restating the basic ideas which have been discussed so far. Then, proceed to the final area if your child shows a desire to accept Jesus.

Repentance is as much a part of a child's conversion as it is an adult's. The point here is to help the child realize that she must repent of her sins. Show the card with the word *repent* on it and ask, Do you know what that word means? (Wait for an answer. She may not know the answer.) At any rate, illustrate the biblical concept of repentance as a change in direction in life. Do this by placing the word *sin* in one part of the room and the word *life* in the opposite direction. Place the child facing the word *sin* and explain that you travel one way in life—toward sin and death or toward Jesus. As the child walks toward sin, show her the picture of Jesus and say: But Jesus came to give you life and He died for your sins. Will you turn from your sins (recall the discussion of *sin*) and turn to Jesus and life? Turning away from sin is what the word *repent* means. Ask, Are you ready and willing to quit doing the things against God which you have been doing? If the answer is yes, then proceed to show the child that her trust must be put in Jesus.

The child may readily say that she trusts Jesus but take a moment to illustrate the idea of trust. Place a chair in front of your child and ask: Do you trust that chair to hold you up? Has it ever failed you before? If you trust it, then show me how you trust it. As the child is sitting in the chair say,"In the same way we show that we trust Jesus by putting ourselves in His care and by doing what He tells us. Are you willing to invite Him into your life as Savior?" Lead the child to pray and ask Jesus to forgive her sins and to come into her life and to be her Savior. Assure your child of God's love and promise by having her repeat John 3:16 with you.

Now say to your child: God has taken your sins away. He has forgiven them because you have trusted Jesus. Write words describing the sins your child named on a small chalkboard and say, God has forgiven you. Erase the words from the board. Or you may list the sins on a piece of paper, tear the paper up, and say: God has torn up the list of your sins and has thrown it away. Now Jesus lives in you.

Lead your child to tell other members of the family about her decision to trust Jesus. Help her understand that this is a natural response to her faith in Jesus.

11

The Lord's People

Joining the church is a big step for anyone, especially a child. The nature of the church and the meaning of church membership are so important that a person should approach such a decision with reverent appreciation for the church.

Children are often introduced into the life of a local church with no basic understanding of what the church is or what the church is supposed to do. Children must be taught correct concepts of the church. This can be done prior to conversion, but it is absolutely essential for the child who has trusted Jesus as Savior. There can be little growth or happiness for the child apart from participation in the privileges and responsibilities of church membership.

Church membership is a natural response to expressing faith in Christ as Savior. The church is important. Your child needs and deserves to have that taught to him.

Session Objectives

There are two primary objectives in this session on the Lord's people. One relates to how the parent can understand the child's concept of the church. The other objective relates to teaching the child certain ideas about the church. The objectives are:

1. To help parents understand the child's concept of the church and lead the child to a more complete understanding of the church.

2. To involve the child in learning activities which will help him understand the concept of the church as people who trust Jesus and who do certain things because they are members of the church.

Major Concepts

Three major ideas or concepts are to be discussed in this session on the church. The ideas are closely interrelated, and each builds upon the preceding one. Think and pray about these ideas until you understand them as a unit. The concepts are: (1) the church is people, (2) the church is special people, and (3) the church is obedient people.

Resources

Pictures. Use pictures of a church building, people worshiping together, a Bible class, and a group of disciples around Jesus.

Words. During this session use the word *church*. Print in bold letters on a 3 by 5 card or piece of paper.

Other. Paper and pencil will be needed.

Bible. Use a version which the child can read easily if you have one.

Procedure

This session on the church is a continuation of the first session on conversion. Take a few minutes to review with your child the basic ideas of sin, the Savior, and the child's response in repentance and faith. This will set a good background for an understanding of the church presented in this session.

Because children are often so literal in their interpretation of the word *church,* we need to be certain that they have not misunderstood the church to be a building. This is often the concept of young children because they hear adults refer to the building as "the church" or "going to church." Watch for this tendency for your child to think this way.

Begin the session by placing pictures in front of the child and asking: What is the church? Which of these is more nearly the church to you? He may choose a picture of a building, a group of people worshiping, or people gathered around Jesus. At any rate, the point is to discover where the child is in his thinking. Ask, Why did you choose that one? Allow time for the answer.

Tell him to keep his picture beside him while both of you see what the Bible says the church is. Have him turn with you to Acts 2:41-42. Explain that Peter had just preached about Jesus as Savior. Have him read verses 41-42 carefully to find out what was added to the church. Emphasize that people received Peter's word and were added to the church. The church is people. Now ask him to look at the picture. Ask: Were you correct? The church is made up of people. Which of these pictures do you think could be like the church? Allow time for discussion, pointing out that the church is people.

After you are certain your child has grasped this concept, move toward the idea that the church is "special people." You may direct discussion by saying: The church is people, but so is a business, a school, or a scout troop. Each is made up of people. Why is the church any different from these things? There are many ways in which the church is special.

Show the picture of Jesus and His disciples and say: The church is special because Jesus started it. Have your child turn to Matthew 16:13-18 and read to you. Explain verses 16-18. Jesus said He would build His church out of people who confessed He was Savior, like Peter did.

Ask, What is so special about church members? Show the picture of people and wait for the answer. If the child has trouble answering, refer again to Acts 2:41 to the words "received his word." Also have the child refer to John 1:12. Emphasize that the church is made up of people who receive Jesus as Savior.

Emphasize that before a person becomes a church member he must repent (turn away) of his sins and trust Jesus as his Savior. This is what is so special about the church. The church is made up of people who have trusted in Jesus as their Savior. They have a new life because God has forgiven them of their sins.

Hold up the word, *church*. Say, "In the New Testament the word for church actually means 'called-out ones,' people called by God to be His special people and to do His special work. So, the church is called for a special purpose. What do you think Jesus wants His church to do?" Allow your child to suggest some actions the church should take.

The purpose now is to help the child realize that the correct response to what Jesus has done is to love Him and to show that love through obedience. Ask, "How do we show Jesus that we love Him and appreciate being a member of His church?" *By doing the things that please him.*) Jesus wants us to put Him first in our lives and to obey Him. Read John 14:15 with your child. Help him see the close connection between love and obedience. Help him see that to obey sometimes is not easy. Sometimes we want to do things other than what Jesus wants us to do. But we show we love Jesus by obeying Him.

Now have your child take a pencil and paper and make a list of things he and other members of the church should do. Here are some Scripture references which may start you on your way: John 15:17; Matthew 28:19-20; Psalm 106:1; Acts 2:42; Ephesians 6:1; Philippians 4:6; Psalm 37:3; 1 Peter 2:21.

There may be several other ideas that should be added to the list. Feel free to let your child make other suggestions which are part of being obedient to Jesus. As you conclude ask: Are you willing to do your part as a church member? Are you willing to obey Jesus?

12

I Want to Be Baptized

Sometimes parents are shocked into concern about their child's spiritual welfare by such a statement as "I want to be baptized." This is, obviously, a request which should be considered. The child means something by his statement. But what does he mean?

He could be saying that he is becoming interested in a religious commitment. Or again, he could be expressing a desire to do what other friends have done. Another reason might be that he sees baptism as an act of obedience and expression of faith in Jesus as Savior. Whatever the case, it is important to know what the child means before he is baptized. Hopefully, this chapter will help you help your child in an understanding of Christian baptism.

Session Objectives

There are two objectives around which this chapter on baptism is developed. They are:

1. To help parents understand their child's concept of baptism and to lead him to a more complete understanding of baptism.

2. To involve the child in learning activities which will

help him understand Christian baptism as an act of obedience and an expression of faith in Jesus as Savior.

Major Concepts

The concepts concerning baptism will be dealt with under the headings: (1) a picture of the gospel, (2) what baptism tells others about you, (3) a promise to God and others, and (4) an act of obedience to God. These concepts are so closely related that you may often find yourself discussing two or more at the same time.

Before proceeding to teach your child, read the following passages and ask yourself some questions. This will help you clarify these concepts in your own understanding.

1. A picture of the gospel. Read Romans 6:4-5. How does Christian baptism show the basic elements of the gospel? What has God done to save us?

2. What baptism tells others about you. Read Romans 6:3-4. Consider the meaning of these phrases "baptized into his death" (v. 3), "walk in newness of life" (v. 4). What does baptism tell others who see you baptized?

3. A promise to God and others. Read Romans 6:6. In baptism, what promise does one make to God and others concerning sin as a way of life?

4. An act of obedience to God. Read the account of Jesus' baptism in Matthew 3:13-17. Jesus came into the world to be the Savior for sinners. His baptism was His open, public commitment to God's will. Jesus sets an example of obedience for us to follow. Also read Acts 2:41. What did those who received Peter's word about Jesus do? How did they show others they were obedient to God's teachings?

Resources

Pictures. (1) A person being baptized is needed. If one is not available, make one by sketching or cutting the picture of a person from a catalog or magazine and placing it on a piece of construction paper with water drawn or colored as a background. (2) Use a picture of Jesus being baptized by John. If this is not available, use a simple picture of Jesus.

Bible. If possible, use a version which a child can read easily.

Procedure

You may have become involved with your child in this session on baptism because you have decided to go through the series of studies. Or you may be discussing baptism as a response to your child's particular interest in being baptized. Whatever the reason, remember to relate baptism to your child's experiences and on a level a child can understand. This session will require thirty to forty-five minutes.

Attempt to be as natural and relaxed as possible and involve your child in discussion early. This will put the child at ease and will help him talk more freely concerning his concept of Christian baptism.

Open the session by relating to your child's experience of seeing someone baptized. Help him recall the experience. Ask, What do you remember about the baptism? Help him identify the reason for the baptism. Ask, Do you know what that person had to do before he could be baptized? (Listen carefully to the answers because they can reveal the insight your child has into baptism. Take time to allow him to clarify his thoughts for you.)

Move now toward a discussion of concept number 1 by saying, Let's look at what the Bible says baptism is. Open the Bible to Romans 6:4-5. Show the picture of a person being baptized. Say: The Bible tells us that baptism is a picture of what God has done to save us. When we are baptized we are showing others the good news about Jesus. Read verses 4-5. Ask, What has Jesus done to save us from sin? Look at verse 4 and help your child see that baptism pictures us "buried" with Christ. Christ died and was buried. Verses 4 and 5 also refer to His resurrection. He was raised from the dead. With a downward gesture of the hand and arm ask, What does it say about Jesus when a person is put under the water? (Allow time for an answer and help clarify the answer if necessary.) With an upward, lifting gesture of hand ask: What does it say about Jesus when a person is brought up out of the water? Allow time for an answer. If this explanation of baptism seems to be beyond your child's ability to understand, use another approach. Emphasize that baptism shows us what Jesus did to save us. Going down into the water means he died and was buried to forgive our sins. Coming up out of the water means he was raised from the dead and gives us life forever. When we are baptiszed, we are saying we believe these things.

Now it is time to proceed toward your child's personal belief in the gospel which baptism pictures. There are two major acts or ideas involved in baptism: immersion (death) and rising (resurrection). Just as these picture something about what Jesus has done, they should also have personal meaning for the person being baptized.

Tie this concept to the one just discussed by asking: Did you know that baptism tells others something about you? What do you think it tells them? Read Romans 6:3-4. Briefly discuss the phrases "baptized into his death" (v. 3) and "walk in newness of life" (v. 4). Baptism shows others that we have personally believed in Christ's death and resurrection to forgive our sins and to give us new life. Illustrate with hand gestures again, saying, Baptism means that Jesus has forgiven our sins and has given us a new life.

Baptism is also a commitment to live for God. The idea of a promise might more readily relate to your child. Ask: Has anyone ever made you a promise? Did they keep the promise? Were you happy or sad? Allow time for answers and explanations to each question. Explain that promises are important and that we should be serious about keeping them. Ask, Did you know that baptism is a promise? Guide your child to look at Romans 6:6 for the promise we make to God and others when we are baptized. Notice especially the idea of not being the servant of sin. Baptism is a promise that we are not going to continue to do those wrong things we did before we trusted Jesus as Savior. Rather, we are promising to do those things which please Jesus. Ask your child to name some things we promise we will do.

Sometimes a child may understand the basic concepts of baptism without realizing it is something God expects of us. If a person has trusted Jesus as Savior, he should be baptized as a way of telling others what Jesus has done for him.

You may begin discussion of this concept by stating: God wants those who trust Him to be baptized. And we are always happier when we do what God wants us to do. Point to the example of Jesus. Use the picture of Jesus' baptism and say, Jesus was baptized to tell everyone He was going to obey the Heavenly Father. Read the account in Matthew 3:13-17. Explain that Jesus sets the example for us to follow. He was baptized to show that He was willing to die for our sins.

Baptism is a natural response for those who have believed in Jesus as Savior. Turn in your Bible to Acts 2:41. Explain the background. Peter, the disciple, had been telling people about how God had sent Jesus to be our Savior and how He had died for our sins and was raised from the dead. Ask your child to read Acts 2:41 and to answer the question: What did those who received Peter's word about Jesus do? (*They were baptized.*) Explain that this is what God would have us to do.

Conclude the session with some questions which focus on the central ideas of the session. Here are some suggestions:

1. What does baptism tell about Jesus?
2. What does baptism tell others about us?
3. What do we promise when we are baptized?

13
The Lord's Supper

"Why can't I take it?"

"Just because you can't, that's why." And so ends the conversation between parent and child until the next time the Lord's Supper is observed in their church.

When can I take it? or Why can't I take it? are questions young children often ask their parents regarding the Lord's Supper. Hopefully, we have more to say than, "Just because you can't."

The Lord's Supper is a fascinating occurrence to children. To be passed by is something of a disappointment. They feel left out. They see other children taking it and may wonder why they are excluded. Thus, the questions which must be answered.

Some children are ready and should be encouraged to participate in the ordinance of the Lord's Supper. However, they should have a basic understanding of the meaning of the observance. You can be of great assistance at this point.

Session Objectives

There are two basic goals which should guide you as you lead your child in this session on the Lord's Supper. They are:

1. To help the parent understand the child's concept of the Lord's Supper and to lead her to a more complete understanding of it.

2. To involve the child in learning activities which will help her understand the Lord's Supper as a message and as an experience or personal commitment.

Major Concepts

The Lord's Supper, sometimes referred to as Communion, has various meanings and implications which are important. Four of those major concepts will be discussed in this session. They are: (1) a picture of the gospel, (2) a time of remembrance, (3) what the Lord's Supper tells others about you, and (4) a time for renewing promises.

Be certain that you understand the concepts before attempting to teach them to your child. Read the suggested passages and attempt to answer the questions concerning each concept.

1. A picture of the gospel. What does the Lord's Supper picture? Read 1 Corinthians 11:23-26.

2. A time of remembrance, What is meant by the command in 1 Corinthians 11:24, "Do this in remembrance of me?" What are we to call to remembrance about Jesus?

3. What the Lord's Supper tells others about you. What

does participation in the Lord's Supper say about the individual's belief in the gospel? Is there a relationship between taking the bread and cup and a prior acceptance of Christ who gave His body and blood for sins?

4. A time for renewing promises. Read 1 Corinthians 11:28. Think about this: the Lord's Supper is a time for examining one's life to see what is right and what is wrong and for renewing our promise to follow Jesus.

Resources

Picture. Use a picture of the Lord's Supper with Jesus and his disciples. One is usually found in most larger Bibles.

Other. Grape juice in a small glass, a piece of bread from which smaller pieces can be broken, paper, and pencil will be needed.

Bible. Preferably, use a version which a child can read easily.

Procedure

If you can arrange for the necessary privacy, the dinner table or a breakfast nook would be the most appropriate place to conduct this session. Such a place usually has an emotional warmth not found in any other part of the house.

Begin with the necessary resources already on the table. Explain that the very first Lord's Supper took place at a table where Jesus was eating a special meal with His disciples. Show the picture of the supper and read the account in Matthew 26:26-29. Explain that what Jesus did made this particular meal even more special. Ask your child to recall two things Jesus did. He broke the bread and passed it to the disciples and told them to eat it. And

He passed the cup to the disciples and told them to drink it.

Ask your child to recall a Lord's Supper service in your church. Ask him to tell you what he saw and what he remembers most about it.

As your child recalls what happened, emphasize that there were two main parts or elements of the supper: bread and drink. Point to these on the table as you talk about them. Ask: What did Jesus say the bread represented or stood for? And what does the cup or drink represent or stand for? Remember here that Jesus used symbolic language: "This is my body (v. 26) and "This is my blood" (v. 28). This can often be interpreted literally by a child. These elements stand for or represent Jesus' body and blood. Be certain your child understands that Jesus was teaching a lesson about what He was going to do for them. He would soon give His body and blood for their sins.

Read the passage in 1 Corinthians 11:24-37. Explain that the apostle Paul was writing to a group of believers, a church, explaining what the Lord's Supper should mean to them. Ask your child to look at the last major phrase of verse 26, "You proclaim the Lord's death until he comes." Ask: What do we proclaim or show that Jesus did when we take the supper? We show that He died for sins.

Now concentrate a few moments on what is meant by the phrase in verse 25, "Do this, as often as you drink it, in remembrance of me." Ask, What are some things we should remember about Jesus when we eat the bread and drink the cup of the Lord's Supper? Your child may suggest several things. Take a piece of paper and write at the top "Things to Remember." Make a brief list as you talk about Jesus and what He did. Your list might include such ideas as the following:

1. Jesus was good to all people.
2. Jesus taught about God.
3. Jesus pleased God by the way He lived.
4. Jesus came into the world as our Savior.
5. Jesus died on the cross to save us from sin and to bring us to God.
6. The bread and drink stand for His death for us.

You may want to briefly read over the list you have compiled. It may be quite appropriate to lead your child to express thanksgiving in prayer for who Jesus was and for what He did. Help your child understand that the Lord's Supper should be a reminder of all these things about Jesus.

Ask your child to tell you what others see when they see you eating the bread and drinking the cup of the Lord's Supper. Help your child understand that others see her as one who has believed in Jesus as Savior. Jesus, through His body, has taken our sins away. Every time we take the Lord's Supper we tell others that Jesus is our Savior and that we live to please Him.

The Lord's Supper is not only a time for remembrance but a time for making our promises to God again. Read 1 Corinthians 11:28. Tell your child that the Lord's Supper is a special time for thinking about what is right and what is wrong in our lives. It is also a time for renewing the promises we have made to God. Ask your child to share some of the promises he or she has made to God. You may want to share some of the promises you have made as you share with your child.

Close the session with a prayer. Ask your child to pray, giving thanks for the Lord's Supper, for what it tells us about Jesus, and for what it tells others about us.

14
Talking with God

One of the unique privileges of a Christian is prayer. It seems almost unbelievable that the God who created and runs this universe would be concerned with the problems of individuals or would hear their prayers. But this is exactly the case! God encourages us to pray to Him and to use prayer as a means of staying in touch with Him.

Our children are taught to pray from the time they are very small. Most of them have been taught to give thanks to God for His good gifts to them. But the prayer life of a child needs to progress beyond giving thanks to incorporate other very important aspects of the Christian life.

The following session on prayer will be an enriching experience for you and your child. As you teach your child about talking with God, you may find that your own prayer life is renewed.

Session Objectives

The two objectives of this session relate to parents' need to understand the child's concept of prayer and expanding upon that concept. The objectives are:

1. To help parents understand their child's concept of

prayer and lead him to a more complete understanding of the purpose and value of prayer.

2. To involve the child in learning activities which will help him understand the basic attitudes of prayer.

Major Concepts

There are many challenging and perplexing aspects of prayer and how it works. But instead of confusing the child with such things about how intercessory prayer works and how God answers prayer, we will confine our session to four basic concepts. The concepts are: (1) The purpose of prayer, (2) learning how to pray, (3) what to pray for, and (4) when and where to pray.

Resources

Bible. Preferably, use a version which the child can read easily.

Other. Paper and pencil will be needed.

Procedure

A good starting place for a discussion on prayer is to consider why prayer is important. You may begin by saying: God tells us to "Pray at all times" (Eph. 6:18). Why do you think God wants us to talk to Him? Listen very carefully to the answers your child gives. What does the answer say about his understanding of the purpose of prayer? Does he think of prayer as a means to change God's mind, to inform God about things that have happened, or of getting things from God?

You may want to begin explaining the purpose of prayer by drawing a human comparison. You may do this in several ways. Here is one suggestion: Your mother (father) and I love you very much and want only the best for you. Sometimes we ask you to do things you don't like to do or understand completely. By doing these things you will become a good person. We want you to trust us always to tell you to do what is best for you. You know, God loves you even more than we do, and He has certain things He wants you to do. Now, how does prayer fit into all of this? (Wait for a response.) Continue: Sometimes it's very hard for us to have the right attitude or to want to do what God wants us to do. What are some things God wants those who trust Him to do? Take a pencil and paper and make a list of things God wants you to do. The list may include such things as: be kind to others, share with others, forgive others, and obey parents.

Now, go back to the purpose of prayer. Hold up the list and ask: Why does God want us to talk with Him? Help your child understand that we pray to God so that He will help us do those things which please Him.

Ask, How do we go about praying in a way which will help us please God? Tell how Jesus' followers came to Him one day and asked Him to teach them to pray. Read Luke 11:1-4. As you come to verse 2, say: "And this is how Jesus taught them to pray." Read the verses and comment that the prayer Jesus taught is much more than just saying words. Tell your child that the words are not as important as our attitude. There are five basic attitudes which should guide our prayers. You may read the major phrases of the prayer and ask after each: What does God want us to think or feel as we pray?

"Father, hallowed be thy name." God is our Father. We are His children through what Jesus has done for us. We should approach God with appreciation and respect.

"Thy kingdom come." To pray "Thy kingdom come" is

to ask that God's loving purpose be done in the world. To pray this means that we are willing for God to have His way in our lives. This is submission to God's will.

"Give us each day our daily bread." This phrase shows that we recognize that God is the Source of all good gifts. In this we express dependence upon God for our most basic needs.

"And forgive us our sins, for we ourselves forgive every one who is indebted to us." To pray this is to recognize that we sin each day. God tells us in 1 John 1:9 that if we admit our sins to God and ask forgiveness He will forgive us. Here forgiveness of others is taught, just as God forgives us.

"And lead us not into temptation." We are in constant need of God's direction if we are to please Him. Here we pray seeking God's direction so that we will not sin against Him.

How does one go about teaching a child to incorporate these ideas into his prayers? First, he must remember the major ideas. You can do this by making a list, "Five Things to Do While Praying." Tell your child to follow this list each time he prays and to talk to God in his own words. The list should be as brief as possible. Here is a suggested list for the child to use.

1. Thank God for making you His child through what Jesus did for you.

2. Tell God that you want to obey Him, even in the things that seem hard for you.

3. Ask God to supply your daily needs, such as food and clothing, and give thanks for them.

4. Tell God that you are sorry for your sins and that you want to forgive those who have hurt you.

5. Ask God to lead you so that you will not sin against Him or others.

Give this list to your child and tell him to use it as a guide until he knows the basic things for which he should pray. This should prove to be a most helpful and practical experience.

The third major concept on prayer is what children should be taught to pray about. A good rule of thumb is to teach the child to pray about anything which concerns him. In this way a child learns that God is concerned about everything that concerns us. A Christian can pray to God about anything. The only condition is that we ask for God's will to be done. You may teach this idea through the following conversation: God is a very special Friend who will listen to us. He tells us in the Bible to tell Him about everything that's bothering us. He says "in everything by prayer . . . let your requests be made known to God" (Phil. 4:6). You can pray about anything that troubles you so long as you always ask God to do what He thinks best.

Now, ask your child to share with you some things about which he will want to pray. Be sensitive to your child's concerns and encourage him to remember to pray for sick friends, national leaders, church leaders, and even those who are not his friends.

One of the most wonderful things about prayer is that we can pray anywhere. It does not have to be a planned time but can be a natural response of the heart at anytime or occasion. However, a specific time teaches the discipline of prayer. Emphasize to your child that each morning he should take a few moments to pray according to the list of suggestions. But tell him that this is not the only time or place to pray.

Ask: What should you do if a classmate at school has made you angry? Should you wait until the next morning to pray about how to act? Why not? (Emphasize that the child can quietly pray in his own heart for the Lord to help him to do the right thing.)

Ask: What if you were told that one of your classmates has been put into the hospital? Should you wait until the next morning to pray for him? Why not? (Emphasize that when we become aware of a need we can pause to ask God's help for others.)

Ask: What if something good happens to you? Do you have to wait until tomorrow to thank God? Why not? (Emphasize that thanksgiving should be expressed when we become aware of God's blessing.)

Close the session with a brief prayer of thanksgiving. Thank God for your child, the time you have spent together, and for the privilege of prayer.

15

A Special Book

The Bible is indeed a special Book. In it one can find the way of salvation, comfort in troubled times, correction from error, and instruction in how to please God (2 Tim. 3:14-17). It is the book of all books and should not be omitted from the lives of our children. Of all the books of which they should be knowledgeable, the Bible should be primary.

The teachings of the Bible stand as the foundation of all Christians profess to believe. However, it is my fear that many who profess to love and cherish the teachings of the Bible never read it. Perhaps the following story illustrates well the truth of many of our lives.

A young mother, home with her preschool-age daughter, was visited by the pastor and his wife. To impress the pastor, the young mother told her daughter to go into another room and get the book "Mommy loves to read." Much to her embarrassment, the child came back with a catalog. The point of this story is that we cannot hope to teach children that "we love to read the Bible" if, in fact, we do not read and apply it. Children learn quickly about what are the priorities in our home.

Timothy's home life was apparently such that he was

taught the importance of the Scriptures from an early age. There are several references to this fact in the letter of 2 Timothy. One particular verse is especially challenging to parents: "From childhood you have been acquainted with the sacred writings which are able to instruct you for salvation through faith in Christ Jesus" (2 Tim. 3:15).

Session Objectives

This session on the Bible will have two major objectives. These objectives should guide the use of all methods and procedures. They are:

1. To help the parent understand the child's concept of what the Bible is and to expand upon that concept.

2. To involve the child in learning activities which will help him understand that the Bible is a special book to be used as a guide for the Christian life.

Major Concepts

There are three major concepts or ideas about the Bible which will be discussed. These concepts are: (1) a special book, (2) doing God's Word, and (3) learning to use the Bible.

To get you to thinking about these ideas prior to the session, consider the following questions:

1. A special book. How is the Bible a special book? What is its role in conversion and Christian growth?

2. Doing God's Word. What should be the ultimate outcome of reading the Bible? Read James 1:22-25.

3. Learning to use the Bible. What are some practical suggestions which can help your child learn how to use the Bible?

Resources

Pictures. Selected pictures from some of the earlier sessions can be used.

Words and references. Print the word *repent* on a 3-by-5 card. Print on a card the reference John 3:16. Other cards with references are: Genesis 1:1; Romans 3:23; Romans 6:23; Psalm 119:105; and Acts 2:41-42.

Other. Two or three children's books will be needed.

Bible. Use a version of the Bible which is easy for your child to read.

Procedure

For this session, consider working at a table where you and the child can lay your Bibles in front of you. This will make it much easier for your child, especially in the Bible activities.

Holding your Bible open in front of you, say, The Bible is a special book. Do you agree with that? (Wait for an answer.) Ask: Why do you say that the Bible is a special book? How is it special to you? (Allow your child time to answer. Reflect with her on the answers she gives.)

Now, guide your child to understand that the Bible is special because it is God's Book. Explain that God wanted all people to know about Him and to love Him. One way He decided to tell people about Himself was through writing. He told different men at different times and places to write what He told them. Some of these men were Moses, King David, Jeremiah, Paul, and Peter. Those who wrote before the birth of Jesus have their writings in the Old Testament. Those who wrote after the birth of Jesus have their writings in the New Testament.

Ask your child to turn in the New Testament to 2 Peter 1:21. Read the verse. Emphasize that the Bible was not written because people saw the need to do it but because God inspired or told them to write it.

Lay other selected books from your child's collection and general books beside the Bible. Ask: How are these books alike? (*Paper, writing, and so forth.*) How is the Bible really different from these other books? (*It is God's Book.*) Explain that these other books may be helpful, but they are not God's Word.

With your Bible open again, say that the Bible is special because of what it tells us. Select some pictures from previous sessions. The point to be made here is that the Bible is a record of who God is and His concern for us. You should choose a few pictures representing the previous sessions. For example, you may choose as one picture from "God, the Loving Creator" a scene of nature. Ask: Where are we told about this? In what book are we told that God made this? (*The Bible.*) Turn with your child to the appropriate reference in Genesis 1 and tell him that the Bible teaches us that God made the world. Try this same procedure with one or more of the pictures from the sessions which utilized pictures. With a little ingenuity, you can make this into a brief review of the sessions already covered. Remember, however, that the idea is to teach that the Bible tells us about God and His concern for us.

A third reason why the Bible is special is that it is a guide to help us please God. Hold up the word *repent* used in session 1. Ask, Do you remember what this means? (Wait for an answer. If the child does not know, remind her that it means to turn from sin to walk toward God.)

Ask, How do you think the Bible can help those who have turned away from sin to please God? The Bible tells us what to do so that we may please God. The idea of a guiding light may help your child remember this idea. Ask your child to imagine himself in a very dark room, so dark he did not know where the door or anything in the room was. Ask, "What would you need in order to see or find your way around the room without getting hurt?"(A flashlight or some kind of light.) Compare this to using the Bible as a guide in our lives. Ask your child to repeat Psalm 119:105, "Thy word is a lamp to my feet and a light to my path." Suggest that she memorize this verse.

Pose this situation: Suppose you were outside in a wooded area, and night started to come. Darkness was everywhere. Before you had left the house you put a flashlight in your pocket. You were in the darkness and did not know which way to go. What would you do?

Certainly you would turn on the flashlight and attempt to find your way back home. What good would the light be if you did not use it?

Emphasize that God's Word is like a light in the darkness. We must obey or do what the Bible teaches in order for it to really benefit us. Ask: What are some things the Bible tells you to do? (*Love others, obey parents, and so forth.*)

Try these situations and allow your child to respond to them:

You are in a store with some friends, and one of them asks you to help him steal some candy. What does the Bible say about stealing? What should you do? (*You shall not steal.*)

Two of your classmates are picking on another and calling her bad names. When you come by, they ask you to join the fun. Can you think of a Bible verse which would guide you? What should you do? (*Be kind one to another.*)

You have a job to do before supper, and your parents depend on you to do it. However, this afternoon there's a special television program which you want to watch. What does the Bible tell you to do? What should you do? (*Obey your parents.*)

The concluding part of this session can be a very helpful and practical experience.

Ask: Do you know what the two main divisions in the Bible are? (*Old Testament and New Testament.*) Have your child find the dividing place. Ask him to remember that all the Old Testament was written before Jesus was born, and all the New Testament was written after Jesus was born.

Turn with your child to the index in the front of the Bible. Show him how the books are arranged in order according to Old Testament and New Testament. Show him also the page number where the books begin. Select a few Old and New Testament books and ask the child to use the index to find them.

Now hold up the card *John 3:16* and talk to your child about this reference. There are three things in this reference which need to be understood. *John* is the name of the book. Allow the child to find this book in the New Testament, using the index. The *3* represents the chapter and is usually found at the head of the chapter. Ask the child to find chapter 3 in John. The number *16* represents the verse. Beginning at the first verse and scanning quickly the child can find the verse. So, John 3:16 is a reference to the Book of John, the third chapter, and the sixteenth verse.

Now try some exercises with other familiar verses: Genesis 1:1; Romans 3:23; Romans 6:23; Psalm 119:105; and Acts 2:41-42. You may need to spell the book names and help your child decide whether the book is in the Old or New Testament.

Encourage your child to read the Bible daily. If she does not already have a reading plan, start her in the Gospel of Mark or some other of the books that are more easily read. Another good approach is for children to use the books *Reading My Bible in Spring, Reading My Bible in Summer, Reading My Bible in Fall, Reading My Bible in Winter* by Lou Heath and Beth Taylor. You can also encourage Bible reading through a family time devoted to that purpose.

16

Growing in the Faith

Almost daily you can read or hear of a mother or father who has abandoned children. Left to fend for themselves, the young children's only hope is that someone will find them before they die from starvation or exposure. Such news angers us. To think that such small children could care for themselves under those conditions is incredible. How could any parent do such a thing?

Yet, there is a spiritual parallel in which some of the best of parents are guilty. They abandon their children spiritually, somehow assuming that once their children have become Christians they can make it on their own. Are such children fully grown? Do they not need encouragement and feeding? Will they come to Christian maturity if we, their parents, abandon them? Or will they die so far as Christian growth is concerned?

The New Testament was written to people who had already become believers in Christ. The main purpose was not to tell the recipients of these letters how to be saved. The primary reason was to challenge the readers to appropriate or apply the new life they possessed to everyday situations—to live as Christians. The writers encouraged, informed, and corrected error, so these Christians might grow in their relationships with the Lord.

Parents occupy a similar position as the New Testament writers. We are to encourage, inform, and correct error so that our children may grow toward spiritual personhood. They are but babes in Christ. We must not, we cannot abandon them.

The Goal of Salvation

Many children are abandoned in the faith because some parents and churches have a very narrow concept of salvation. They hold that people are saved in order to go to heaven. But that is only a partial answer as to why God saves anyone.

Those who feel that the only real benefit of salvation is a future one have not fully understood the biblical goal of God's redeeming love. Such a concept may also cause parents to feel that nothing else is important beyond their child's being saved. "He's saved," they say, "and that's all that matters." Is that *all* that matters?

Somewhere we need to ask what God's goal is for those whom He saves. What does God purpose for those whom He saves?

Simply stated, God has called all who believe to be like Jesus. In the Roman letter, Paul referred to this as being "conformed to the image of his Son" (Rom. 8:29). Obviously, there is much more to salvation than the future aspect of heaven. Our concern, here and now, should be to grow to be like Jesus. This is the lifetime, all-encompassing, goal of each person who becomes a Christian. This was the aspiration of the apostle Paul, expressed in Philippians 3:14, "I press on toward the goal for the prize of the upward call of God in Christ Jesus." Anything less is unworthy of the salvation God has provided through Christ.

Once a child has trusted Jesus as Savior, we should attempt to keep him in the way which leads toward the goal of salvation. The remainder of this chapter will present some practical suggestions as to how we can do this.

Growing in the Faith

There are many subjects which could fall into the scope of practical suggestions to keep a child growing in the faith. The following are only some of the most obvious ones. Instead of an exhaustive treatment of each subject, the discussion will only serve as a starter for parents.

Communication

Perhaps the key to helping your child in the faith is to maintain a relationship in which the child feels a freedom to talk about any subject with you. Work on maintaining your relationship through each stage of your child's growth. Listen as much as you talk. Spend time as a family in activities your whole family enjoys. Being in touch with your child spiritually will depend largely on whether he feels free to communicate with you about his doubts, misgivings, confusion, and victories.

Personal Example

The old adage that religion is more caught than taught has a certain ring of truth to it. Children do not expect their parents to be perfect, but they do expect them to be consistent. Religious values are much more meaningful to children if they are supported by parental example. Parents who expect to keep their children faithful to the

Lord while being unfaithful themselves are like the blind leading the blind (Matt. 15:14).

Such practices as Bible reading, church attendance, prayer, giving, and acts of kindness impress children much more than talk. Yet, there must be the spirit of love and selflessness which characterize such acts, or they become empty and hollow. Religious acts without the right attitude teach children to try to "buy God off" by doing a good deed.

The Battle Within

Your child needs to be made aware that sin is still a real possibility for him. As a matter of fact, he will sin. His desire should be to please God and not to sin; but there is still the will to do wrong which remains even after God, the Holy Spirit, comes to live within him. Many times Satan will tempt him to do things which are wrong, but the Holy Spirit wants him to obey God. At this time, the child will feel drawn in two different directions. The child should be taught that he has a choice. He does not have to do the wrong thing. God will help your child do the right thing if he will ask God to help.

Satan and Temptation

You perhaps have seen the T-shirt some people wear which declares, "The devil made me do it." Satan is so often blamed for what is human responsibility. In the course of human history, Satan has never made one person, other than himself, to sin. The devil tempts us at our point of weakness, but we choose to sin. James 4:7 teaches us that we have power over Satan if we so choose, "Resist the devil and he will flee from you." A prayer to God, singing a familiar hymn, or quoting an appropriate verse of Scripture will usually drive Satan away.

Temptation is the work of Satan. He wants us to sin but cannot make us do so. He makes sin look good and sometimes makes us think to obey him will be good for us. Sin is certainly easier at times than obeying God because Satan appeals to our weakest areas.

Help your child determine what his weaknesses are so that he can be on guard for Satan. Perhaps he has an explosive temper, is prideful, or selfish. Teach your child that temptation is not sin but to choose to do what you are tempted to do is sin.

Two pieces of practical advice need to be given about temptation. First, your child should be told that he can put himself into situations where sin comes very easily. It is not fair to expect God to keep us from sin if we deliberately put ourselves in tempting situations. For instance, the habits of talk and action of some children should make them less likely friends of the Christian child. This is not snobbery but is recognition of how associates can influence one. Another example could be that the child who prepares well for an exam has no reason to cheat. If he does not take responsibility to do his studying, he opens himself to the possible temptation to cheat rather than to fail the exam.

Second, your child needs to know how to encounter new situations of which he is morally unsure. A good rule to follow is: "If you don't know, don't do it."

What to Do When You Sin

One of the most disconcerting and discouraging discoveries to a new Christian is that he can and does sin. The knowledge that he has sinned brings guilt and a sense of doubt about his relationship to the Lord. What should a person do when he realizes he has sinned? He should acknowledge it to himself, confess it to God, and ask forgiveness. Teach your child to remember this concept as it is expressed in 1 John 1:9: "If we confess our sins, he is faithful and just, and will forgive our sins and cleanse us from all unrighteousness." Once your child has confessed his sin to God, he is no longer guilty and should not worry about guilt.

Do the Good You Know to Do

Refraining from doing evil is not the only side of the Christian faith. To pull undesired weeds from a flower bed does not assure the growth of flowers. The seed must be planted, watered, fed, and cultivated. Likewise, the goal of the Christian life is not reached by refraining from doing certain things.

The Christian life is not rules and regulations. It is living in obedience to what God tells us to do. This, God tells us in the Bible and by the impression of the Holy Spirit. You can help your child immeasurably by teaching him things that he should do as a Christian. Teach him to express love, consideration, and forgiveness for others. Teach him to be caring and concerned about the welfare of others. Teach him to take responsibility for his own actions. These are all characteristics of Jesus.

The Church

Your church can play a vital role in supplementing your teaching as a Christian parent. Your child can benefit greatly through friendships and study at such activities as Sunday School, training organizations, missions organizations, and music activities. But do not assume that these will take the place of what you, the parent, ought to do.

You should have an understanding in your home that Sunday is a day of worship. If parents take the lead in this, children usually follow without much fuss. Keeping your children in church where they are constantly exposed to expressions of the Christian faith and people who live the Christian faith can do much to keep them in the Way.

Proverbs 22:6 should challege every parent to do his best in teaching about God. "Train up a child in the way he should go,and when he is old he will not depart from it." This is not merely a reference to church attendance but to a relationship where parents take their teaching role seriously. If children are taught the Christian faith by a real Christian, it is unlikely that any other philosophy could hold them very long. Truth revealed through the personality of a parent has an immeasurable, eternal effect upon a child.